DEAR GREEN MARKETER

*Fresh Ideas for Marketing Green Products
to a Public that Doesn't Seem to Care*

JEFF DUBIN

ISBN: 1460992040
ISBN 13: 9781460992043

For my wife Allison, my parents, and everyone else who has encouraged me to pursue my dreams.

TABLE OF CONTENTS

DATA DEEP DIVES

INTRODUCTION

While farmers' markets and Prius sales are humming along now, household product makers like Clorox just can't seem to persuade mainstream customers to buy green again.

*(**The New York Times**, April 21, 2011)*

The green marketing battlefield is littered with the corpses of sustainable products that didn't make it as well as scores of the walking wounded. Sure, it's tough for green right now. We have a recession that is officially over but don't tell that to those still seeking a job or those with jobs that pay a lot less than people are used to making. And then there are many Americans who are in strong shape financially but who have been sobered by the events of the past few years. Green brands, whether actually premium priced or just saddled with that perception, are definitely fighting strong headwinds.

Financial problems have not only hit Americans in the pocketbook but they have also made us preoccupied with money. The stock market. The federal budget deficit. Cuts to basic services. Cuts in our own spending. Who has the mental bandwidth to think about the environment?

A final reason green products face rough sledding is that the environmental benefits these products purport to provide just aren't seen as needed by many Americans. A steady drumbeat of doubts about global warming from right wing pundits and politicians has spread throughout the body politic. And record cold and snow in many parts of the US in the winter of 2011 coupled with a freak October snowstorm in the northeast doesn't look like global warming to many Americans. The difference between the phrases "global warming" and "climate change" is just esoteric semantics to many Americans.

And yet I'm guardedly optimistic about the future of sustainable brands. Despite missteps, the number of green brands continues to grow. And corporate behemoths like Walmart have taken up the green banner. Most important, **there is so much more makers of sustainable products can do** to engage people's environmental concerns and execute on marketing basics more effectively by making people aware of firms' eco-friendly offerings and convincing people they work and are reasonably priced.

The essays in this book address the steps green marketers can take to maximize the success of their products, helping both their bottom lines and potentially our planet as well. These essays appeared as blog posts on my company's (Green Meridian) website as well as other websites. They are based in part on the results of the *Sustainability in the Mainstream* marketing research study we issued in 2010 to shine a light on women's purchasing of green household cleaners and personal care products. However, I want to provide more than neat marketing research stats. **I want to challenge the green marketing community to do things differently.**

For those that want to dig into the data, I've liberally sprinkled data from the *Sustainability in the Mainstream* study throughout the book. These *Data Deep Dives* will provide additional pearls of insight for those of you that want to explore an issue further.

I'd love to hear what you think about the ideas presented here. Please do not hesitate to contact me at Jeff.Dubin@greenmeridian.com if you want to give me a piece of your mind. You may not agree with everything I've written but at the very least I hope this book will provoke and stimulate.

Happy reading!

Princeton, NJ

February 2012

I

POTHOLES IN THE ROAD TO GREEN

I Know It's Better for the Environment But...

It seems like a no-brainer. All other things being equal, why *wouldn't* consumers prefer green products over non-green ones? In the eyes of many women, though, all other things (a.k.a. more conventional product features such as price) are *not equal*. First let's look at the case of household cleaners to see what these "other things" are exactly. In a study with 628 women, Green Meridian found that how well a cleaner works (seen as very important by 87%), price (78%), smell (62%), availability where women shop (53%), and how healthful a cleaner is (50%) were the cleaner features women most frequently consider when purchasing a cleaner. [See Data Deep Dive #1 for more details.]

So how did women rate green household cleaners vs. their non-green competitors on these key product features? And the results are....

Perceptions of Green vs. Non-Green Cleaners

Cleaner Feature	Winner
Effectiveness	Draw
Price	Non-green
Smell	Green
Availability	Non-green
Healthfulness	Green

[See Data Deep Dive #2 for more details.]

So why don't green household cleaners have a larger market share?

These results are not bad for green cleaners considering that non-green household cleaners still have the lion's share of the cleaner market. The optimist will say, "There's a lot of potential for green household cleaner sales to grow." The more negative person, however, might wonder why green cleaners aren't selling better when perceptions of them are decent.

Well, here are a few ideas:

- <u>Poor awareness</u>: Women are still far more aware of non-green brands than of green ones.

- <u>Loyalty elsewhere</u>: Many women have an attachment to the non-green household cleaners they've used for years. With these women, the green upstarts have to blow the door off its hinges to supplant tried and true non-green brands that in many cases were used by these women's mothers and their mothers' mothers.

- <u>Green still seen as falling short on the basics</u>: For many women, green brands' positives are eclipsed by perceived shortcomings on key conventional features.

Winning some battles with the least green women but losing the war

Let's look more closely at that last point. Green Meridian found in its *Sustainability in the Mainstream* study that approximately half the market is composed of women we call *Non-Greens,* women who buy green household cleaners and personal care products 15% or less of the time. *Non-Greens* typically consider fewer product features than their greener peers when buying household cleaners. Basically, these women are just considering product effectiveness (cited by 84% of *Non-Greens* as very important), price (78%), smell (58%), and availability (47%). [See Data Deep Dive #3 for more details.]

On three of these four cleaner features *Non-Green,* women deemed non-green products to be superior. Rut roh. Green products fared ok on smell, on which they are viewed similarly to non-green products. No wonder *Non-Greens* are non-green.

And on the other end of the green purchasing spectrum...

The greenest 22% of women we call *Frequent Green Purchasers.* These women put a lot of thought into the cleaners they buy. At least half of *Frequent Greens* cited nine different product features as being very important when they buy cleaners, including conventional features as well as products' impact on the environment. And *Frequent Greens* were positive about green cleaners' performance on all nine. What a difference from the *Non-Greens!*

In the middle of the green purchasing spectrum are the *Moderate Greens* and their product opinions are mixed. First, the good news for green marketers: many of the women in this group, which comprise 30% of the women surveyed, consider a product's healthfulness when purchasing household cleaners. And these women typically consider green products to be more healthful. Also, *Moderate Greens* saw green products as superior on smell. However, they viewed sustainable cleaners as about equal to their non-green competitors on effectiveness. And now the bad news: the *Moderate Greens* often saw green products as more expensive and less available than non-green ones.

So let's end on an optimistic note. With the women who are moderate or heavy purchasers of green cleaners, green products are already seen more favorably on at least some conventional product features, particularly smell. Add to that green's strongly perceived superiority on healthfulness and environmental impact, and we have a strong foundation on which to grow green household cleaner use. The keys are:

☑ Increasing women's awareness of green cleaner brands

☑ Bolstering consumers' perceptions of their price, availability, and effectiveness

As far as the less green half of the women in the market, marketers of sustainable products face a much tougher battle to win hearts and wallets.

Data Deep Dive #1

Stated Importance of Factors Affecting Household Cleaner Selection

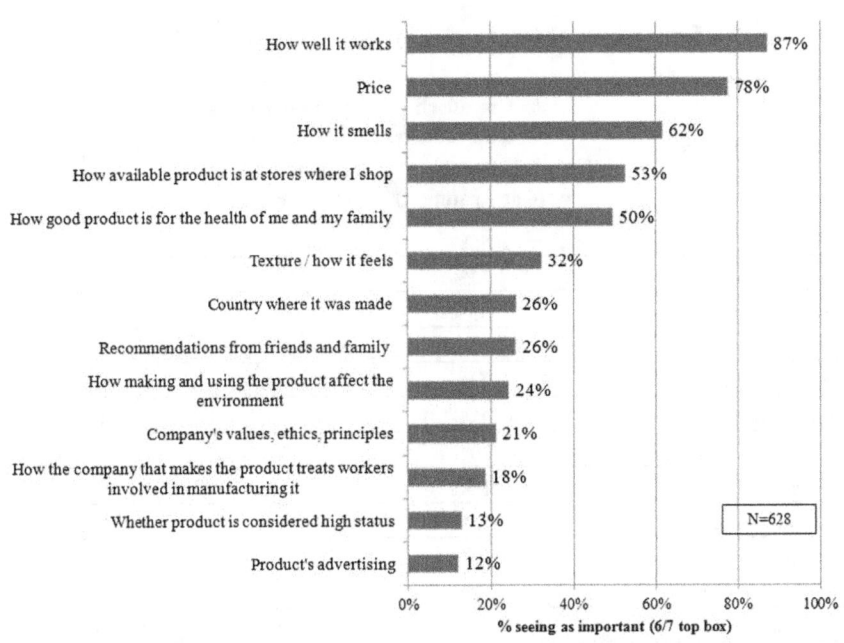

Data Deep Dive #2

Perceptions of Green vs. Non-Green Household Cleaners.

Perceptions of Green vs. Non-Green Household Cleaners

N=628	% Considering Green Products Better (6 or 7 ratings*)	% Considering Non-Green Products Better (1 or 2 ratings*)	Difference
Effect on environment	58%	6%	52%
Healthfulness	55%	6%	49%
Company's values	35%	6%	29%
Treatment of workers	25%	5%	20%
Perceived status	24%	9%	14%
How it smells	27%	13%	14%
Country where made	20%	7%	13%
Texture	17%	9%	8%
Recommendations	16%	13%	3%
Advertising	12%	13%	-1%
How well it works	18%	20%	-2%
Availability	15%	28%	-13%
Price	16%	38%	-22%

*On a 1-7 scale

Data Deep Dive #3A

% of Each Green Purchasing Group Saying Cleaner Feature is Important

	Total Population (n=628)	Non-Greens (n=301)	Moderate Greens (n=191)	Frequent Greens (n=136)
		A	B	C
How well it works	86.5%	84.0%ₐ	88.5%ₐ	89.3%ₐ
Price	77.6%	77.9%ₐ	79.6%ₐ	74.0%ₐ
How it smells	61.6%	58.1%ₐ	64.7%ₐ	65.0%ₐ
How available product is in the stores where I shop	52.5%	47.3%ₐ	56.4%ₐ	58.6%ₐ
How good product is for the health of me and my family	49.5%	32.7%ₐ	54.6%ᵦ	79.9%꜀
Texture / how it feels	32.3%	23.7%ₐ	34.3%ᵦ	48.6%꜀
Country where it was made	26.1%	13.1%ₐ	29.4%ᵦ	50.6%꜀
Recommendations from friends and family	26.0%	23.3%ₐ	23.0%ₐ	36.2%ᵦ
How making and using the product affect the environment	24.3%	3.9%ₐ	30.2%ᵦ	61.6%꜀
Company's values, ethics, principles	21.1%	9.1%ₐ	21.6%ᵦ	47.0%꜀
How the company that makes the product treats workers	18.5%	6.8%ₐ	21.5%ᵦ	40.2%꜀
Whether product is considered high status	12.8%	8.5%ₐ	10.4%ₐ	25.6%ᵦ
Product's advertising	12.1%	8.4%ₐ	14.0%ₐ,ᵦ	17.4%ᵦ

Results are based on two-sided tests with significance level 0.05. For each significant pair, the key of the category with the smaller column proportion appears under the category with the larger column proportion. Tests are adjusted for all pairwise comparisons within a row of each innermost subtable using the Bonferroni correction.

 **Data Deep Dive #3B**

% of Each Green Purchasing Group Saying Personal Care Feature is Important

	Total Population (n=628)	Non-Greens (n=301)	Moderate Greens (n=191)	Frequent Greens (n=136)
		A	B	C
How well it works	87.0%	86.7%$_a$	86.2%$_a$	89.0%$_a$
Price	80.0%	80.1%$_a$	83.2%$_a$	75.3%$_a$
How it smells	71.9%	70.5%$_a$	71.5%$_a$	75.5%$_a$
How good product is for the health of me and my family	57.2%	43.3%$_a$	64.9%$_b$	77.0%$_b$
How available product is in the stores where I shop	54.9%	53.9%$_a$	53.5%$_a$	59.3%$_a$
Texture / how it feels	52.0%	46.1%$_a$	53.2%$_{a,b}$	63.3%$_b$
Recommendations from friends and family	31.8%	29.1%$_a$	30.5%$_a$	39.7%$_a$
How making and using the product affect the environment	26.9%	6.1%$_a$	34.4%$_b$	62.6%$_c$
Country where it was made	24.5%	11.7%$_a$	24.2%$_b$	53.3%$_c$
Company's values, ethics, principles	23.2%	7.8%$_a$	28.2%$_b$	50.3%$_c$
How the company that makes the product treats workers involved in manufacturing it	20.6%	9.2%$_a$	24.1%$_b$	41.0%$_c$
Whether product is considered high status	15.5%	9.2%$_a$	17.1%$_b$	27.3%$_b$
Product's advertising	12.9%	10.8%$_a$	13.7%$_a$	16.6%$_a$

Results are based on two-sided tests with significance level 0.05. For each significant pair, the key of the category with the smaller column proportion appears under the category with the larger column proportion. Tests are adjusted for all pairwise comparisons within a row of each innermost subtable using the Bonferroni correction.

FOR MANY AMERICAN WOMEN, GREEN BRANDS ARE MIA

Woody Allen famously once said, "Eighty percent of success is showing up." Perhaps the same can be said of consumer brands. Before green marketers can fight the battle of perceptions in the consumer's mind, they first have to make sure their brands exist there. And data from my firm Green Meridian's study, *Sustainability in the Mainstream,* suggests that in terms of consumer awareness green household cleaner and personal care product brands are often missing in action.

Only 35% of the women surveyed were able to name even just one green household cleaner brand off the top of their heads. The situation is even more discouraging for green personal care products, with *just 18%* of women successfully naming one green personal care brand without any prompting. [See Data Deep Dives #4 and #5 for more details.]

In follow-up in-person interviews, a solid majority of the women interviewed did not recognize many green brands even when shown the goods. For instance, when presented with sample Green Works products, women typically zeroed in on the familiar Clorox logo but the Green Works name often elicited blank stares.

Disconnection from green

Women see a trio of "disconnection factors" - low green brand awareness, poor availability, and limited product variety – as major reasons why they are not purchasing more green products. (And not surprisingly, the high cost of green products was the most frequently cited obstacle to buying green).

And nowhere is the disconnection problem more evident than with the women where the opportunity to expand green product use is greatest. 26% of the women surveyed in the *Sustainability in the Mainstream* study currently purchase green products a low to moderate amount but also said they would like to buy more green products in the future. This group, whom we've dubbed *Green Aspirants*, represents a potential goldmine from which green marketers can attract more mainstream customers. So what do *Green Aspirants* say is holding them back from greening their purchases?

After high cost, three of the next four obstacles to buying green household cleaners most often cited by *Green Aspirants* were poor availability, low awareness, and limited product variety. And it is also important to note that *Green Aspirants* feel *more disconnected* than *both* those less frequent green purchasers that don't aspire to be more green *as well as* those women who are more frequent purchasers of green products. In essence, the *Green Aspirants* are stranded with a bunch of needs and wants that they can't act upon. [See Data Deep Dive #6 for more details.]

For personal care products, *Green Aspirants* are even more emphatic in citing poor access and awareness as blocking their path to greater greenness. [See Data Deep Dive #7 for more details.]

So, in short, we have a group of less green women who want to green their purchasing but who so far have been unable to do so.

So what's a green marketer to do?

Connect, connect, connect! While racing to win the war of perceptions with non-green products smack in the middle of the standard product adoption process, green marketers must not neglect both the beginning and end of the process (shown below). With many people not aware of green brands, green marketers are talking and the greenest consumers are often the only people that can hear them. That's unfortunate because there are other consumers that might increase their green purchases if also brought into the conversation. Consumer disconnection is also taking its toll on green product sales at the end of the adoption process, where trial and use are stymied by poor green product availability in the stores where *Green Aspirants* shop.

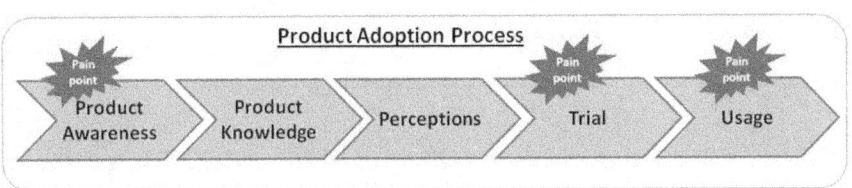

 **Data Deep Dive #4**

Unaided Awareness of Green Household Cleaner Brands

Brand/Company	% Women Mentioning (n=628)
Green Works	17.2%
Clorox	9.9%
Simple Green	8.4%
Method	4.1%
Seventh Generation	4.0%
Windex	3.2%
Various non-green brands	3.1%
Arm & Hammer	2.8%
Lysol	2.0%
Other (20 Mule Team Borax	1.8%
Melaleuca/Sol-U-Mel/Ecosense	1.2%
Shaklee	1.1%
Store brands (Safeway, Bright Green, Kirkland)	1.0%
Home remedies (vinegar, baking soda)	1.0%
Tide	0.9%
Mean Green	0.8%
Earth Friendly/ECOS	0.8%
Scrubbing Bubbles	0.7%
Orange Glo	0.6%
EcoDiscoveries	0.6%
Nature's Source	0.6%
Mr. Clean	0.5%
365 (Whole Foods)	0.5%
Johnson & Johnson	0.5%
Mrs. Meyers	0.3%
BioKleen	0.3%
Sun & Earth	0.2%

 # Data Deep Dive #5

Unaided Awareness of Green Personal Care Product Brands

Brand/Company	% Women Mentioning (n=628)
Variety of green brands*	4.2%
Burt's Bees	3.6%
Various non-green brands	3.6%
Aveeno	2.2%
Tom's of Maine	1.9%
Green store brands	1.8%
Almay	1.6%
Bare Escentuals (Bare Minerals)	1.5%
Dove	1.3%
Arm & Hammer	1.3%
Suave	1.3%
Melaleuca/Sol-U-Mel/Ecosense	1.0%
Jason	1.0%
Origins	0.7%
Oil of Olay	0.7%
Pantene	0.7%
Aveda	0.6%
365 (Whole Foods)	0.6%
Method	0.6%
Neutrogena	0.6%
Avon	0.5%
Home remedies	0.5%
Colgate/Crest	0.5%
Garnier	0.4%
Shaklee	0.4%
Herbal Essences	0.4%
Biolage Matrix	0.4%

Data Deep Dive #6

% of Each Green Intention Group Citing as a Barrier to Green Cleaner Purchase

% agreeing with barrier	Barrier Type*	Total Population (n=615)	Status Quo's (n=332)	Green Aspirants (n=160)	Frequent Greens (n=123)
			A	B	C
Green household cleaners are too expensive	P	55.7%	56.4%$_a$	64.0%$_a$	42.9%$_b$
Green household cleaners don't work as well.	Q	34.3%	34.5%$_a$	39.6%$_a$	27.1%$_a$
Green household cleaners are hard to find.	A	31.2%	23.8%$_a$	46.6%$_b$	31.0%$_a$
I like the 'non-green' cleaners I already use.	Q	30.5%	34.7%$_a$	28.2%$_{a,b}$	22.3%$_b$
I'm not aware of many green household cleaners.	A	28.2%	25.2%$_a$	38.4%$_b$	23.2%$_a$
The variety of green household cleaners is poor.	A	24.1%	22.2%$_a$	33.1%$_b$	17.6%$_a$
Not sure green cleaners are better for health.	S	23.6%	23.3%$_a$	27.1%$_a$	20.1%$_a$
Green household cleaners don't smell as good.	Q	18.1%	20.6%$_a$	19.2%$_{a,b}$	10.2%$_b$
I would really have to change my lifestyle.	L	17.5%	15.7%$_a$	19.0%$_a$	20.4%$_a$
Don't trust companies say their cleaners are green.	S	17.2%	14.3%$_a$	20.3%$_a$	21.1%$_a$
I have other things to worry about.	L	16.0%	14.5%$_a$	14.3%$_a$	22.4%$_a$
Buying green cleaners won't make much of a diff.	S	14.4%	13.6%$_a$	16.7%$_a$	13.5%$_a$
Environmental problems aren't as bad as they say.	S	13.1%	12.2%$_a$	15.3%$_a$	13.0%$_a$
My friends & family don't use green cleaners.	L	9.4%	8.5%$_a$	9.0%$_a$	12.2%$_a$
Being green is for hippies.	L	6.2%	5.6%$_a$	8.5%$_a$	4.6%$_a$

Results are based on two-sided tests with significance level 0.05. For each significant pair, the key of the category with the smaller column proportion appears under the category with the larger column proportion. Tests are adjusted for all pairwise comparisons within a row of each innermost subtable using the Bonferroni correction.

*P=Price, Q=Product Quality, A=Access, S=Green Skepticism, L=Lifestyle

 # Data Deep Dive #7

% of Each Green Intention Group Citing as a Barrier to Personal Care Purchase

% agreeing with barrier	Barrier Type*	Total Population (n=628)	Status Quo's (n=332)	Green Aspirants (n=160)	Frequent Greens (n=136)
			A	B	C
Green personal care products are too expensive.	P	53.4%	55.8%a	61.1%a	38.5%b
Green personal care products are hard to find in the stores where I shop.	A	36.5%	30.1%a	55.7%b	29.3%a
I'm not aware of many green personal care products.	A	35.4%	35.2%a	50.6%b	17.6%c
I like the 'non-green' personal care products I already use.	A	33.1%	38.7%a	34.1%a	18.1%b
The variety of green personal care products is poor.	Q	33.0%	27.5%a	52.6%b	23.3%a
Green personal care products don't work as well.	Q	31.4%	34.3%a	31.8%a	23.8%a
I'm not sure green personal care products are better for the health of my family and me.	S	25.6%	26.0%a	29.1%a	20.3%a
I would really have to change my lifestyle to buy more green personal care products.	Q	19.1%	19.5%a	21.8%a	15.1%a
Green personal care products don't smell as good.	L	17.3%	15.6%a	21.3%a	16.7%a
I don't trust companies that say their personal care products are green.	S	16.8%	15.1%a	21.9%a	14.9%a
I have other things to worry about besides the environment.	S	16.0%	20.0%a	14.9%a,b	7.4%b
Environmental problems aren't as bad as they say.	L	14.5%	13.2%a	14.4%a	18.0%a
Green personal care products don't look as good.	S	12.8%	11.5%a	17.1%a	10.9%a
Buying green personal care products won't make much of a difference.	Q	12.5%	10.9%a	15.6%a	13.0%a
My friends and family don't use green personal care products.	L	10.9%	10.3%a	9.9%a	13.9%a
Being green is for luppies.	L	3.9%	2.3%a	4.2%a,b	7.5%b

Results are based on two-sided tests with significance level 0.05. For each significant pair, the key of the category with the smaller column proportion appears under the category with the larger column proportion. Tests are adjusted for all pairwise comparisons within a row of each innermost subtable using the Bonferroni correction.

*P=Price, Q=Product Quality, A=Access, S=Green Skepticism, L=Lifestyle

For Some, Green
Just Means Moldy

Familiarity may breed contempt but with green products it's outdated familiarity (i.e., circa 1973) that may be breeding contempt. Green Meridian's *Sustainability in the Mainstream* marketing research study compared how women with limited access to green products (i.e., those seeing poor green product availability as a barrier preventing them from buying more green products) view green products on a variety of features with women that don't feel so cut off. The study found that **women that have trouble obtaining green products viewed them more negatively than their better connected counterparts.**

In particular, 52% of the so-called disconnected women saw non-green household cleaners as superior to green ones on price while *only 28%* of the "connected" women said that non-green cleaners were priced better than green ones. Even with a feature as concrete as price, perceptions can vary greatly among consumers. A similar, although less pronounced, dynamic was observed with women's perceptions of green product effectiveness. On the other hand, perceptions of green product smell and texture vary little by how easy it is for women to buy green goods. [See Data Deep Dives #8 and #9 for more details.]

By the way, effectiveness and price were two of the product features most frequently mentioned by women as the ones they use to select household cleaners. So differences in perceptions of these features really matter.

Old, unchallenged memories

So how on earth are "green-detached" women arriving at their impressions of green products? Their opinions may be shaped to some extent by old experiences that may not square with today's natural product realities. Green marketing guru Jacquie Ottman in her book *Green Marketing* says:

> *Gone are the dimly lit general-type stores with cluttered aisles, bulk bins, and limp organic vegetables. In their place are scores of cheery health-food and specialty stores that carry a dizzying array of branded natural foods and green general merchandise.*

Although many of these hippie stores may be gone, memories of them can have strong staying power, particularly for consumers that are Baby Boomers. Also, many product categories have experienced an influx of green products only recently and people's green product impressions may be based on their experiences with one or two older products. So green products for some people are caught in a time warp much like our remembering someone in high school as a perpetually stoned slacker even though now they are a hardworking professional with 2.5 kids, a white picket fence, and... you get the picture. If you don't meet the person now, your memory of the person occupies for eternity the little compartment in the back of your brain reserved for impressions of her.

Like our enduring memories of the high school classmates we haven't seen in years, the outsize influence of our dated perceptions of so-called forerunner products, such as green products from the '70s and '80s, has been documented by researchers. In a 1988 paper that appeared in *Advances in Consumer Research*, Professors Gregory Carpenter (now at Northwestern) and Kent Nakamoto (now at Virginia Tech) suggested "that, in many cases, early entrants frame the consumer's perceptions of [a] product category, thereby defining the rules of competition."

Remember Psych 101?

For green marketers to effectively counteract the negative green product perceptions bequeathed by the green products of yesteryear, marketers have to understand the psychological forces giving these products so much power over people's minds. So what forces may be operating in the unconscious of women who are isolated from green products?

- *Primacy effect* refers to the tendency for the first information received about a person, place, or thing to carry more weight than later information.

- Although *stereotypes* are often discussed in terms of unconscious biases we have about certain groups of people, we can also extend this concept to how some people feel about green products. Where do stereotypes come from? Cognitive psychology theory holds that connections between people, products, etc. and perceptions made often enough in the conscious mind eventually become unconscious. According to Yale social psychologist John Bargh, stereotype formation is particularly prevalent in situations where "conscious choice and decision making are *not* needed." Perceptions of green products and organic food co-ops have formed and entered the unconscious of many people because they have not been needed in most people's daily decision making. The challenge for green marketers is how to challenge stereotypes that have been locked away in the vault of the unconscious for so many years.

- *Familiarity bias* is a preference for the familiar. According to an August 2008 article by a group of Jacksonville University researchers, "When making a purchasing decision, consumer confidence is usually higher if familiarity with a particular brand is higher." Score a point for the cliché, "To know me is to love me."

- *Loss aversion* posits that humans have a greater desire to avoid losses than to experience comparable gains. Many women feel that any potential health and environmental benefits from using green products are outweighed by the potential to be lighter in the wallet and saddled with a product that doesn't work.

Challenging green stereotypes

Fortunately, academics have uncovered a few effective ways to combat negative perceptions:

- <u>Directly attack perceived deficiencies</u>: According to Carpenter and Nakamoto, perceptions of a type of product can be changed when experience with these products is limited. Think of the impressionable young child vs. the curmudgeonly man set in his ways. That means that effective marketing has a chance to substantially change long-held conceptions of green products among those people who have little experience with them. And research and marketers' experience show that it pays to be direct.

Drugmaker Allergan did just that in 2007 when it tackled the common stereotype of Botox causing "face freeze." In response, the company launched an advertising campaign dubbed "Freedom of Expression."

- Expose yourself: Psychotherapists use "exposure therapy" to treat anxiety disorders with the idea that repeated exposure to the source of anxiety will ultimately lessen the source's ability to generate anxiety. In the same way, repeated exposure to green products may make them seem less foreign, challenging stereotypes and weakening the familiarity bias that has led many women to view green products less favorably. Mainstream consumers need a risk-free way to get to know green products. Offering trial-sized samples is key.

- Gain credibility through reviews in mainstream publications: Professors Mogilner (Wharton), Vohs (Minnesota), and Aaker (Stanford) have studied the stereotypes people have of nonprofit firms, an analogous situation to green products. Like their green product counterparts, nonprofits are typically viewed as "warmer" than for-profit companies but they are also viewed as less competent. One way to compensate for this competence gap, they found, was to be favorably reviewed in an established mainstream publication like *The Wall Street Journal*. Likewise, less green women would likely be more swayed by a favorable sustainable lipstick review in *Vogue*, say, than one in *Greener Living*.

In short, negative product opinions have a strong hold on people's minds when they've been lodged in them for years but they can be dislodged by bringing them out into the light and challenging them.

Data Deep Dive #8

Green Cleaner Access Issues vs. Product Perceptions

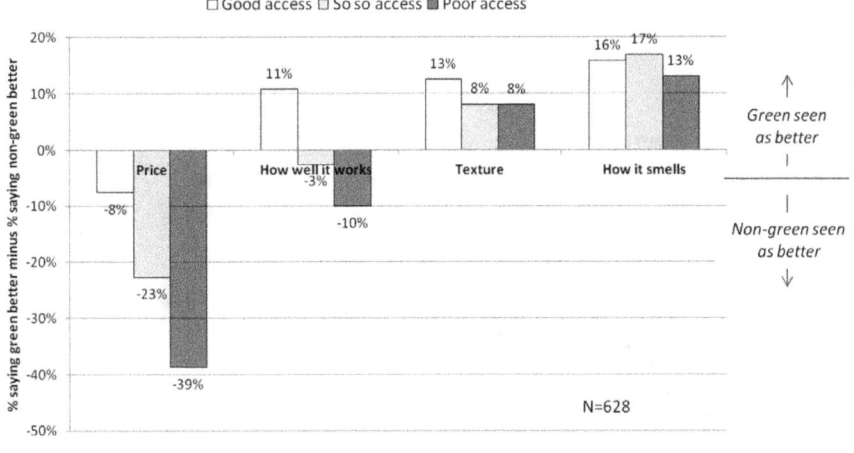

Data Deep Dive #9

Green Personal Care Product Access Issues vs. Product Perceptions

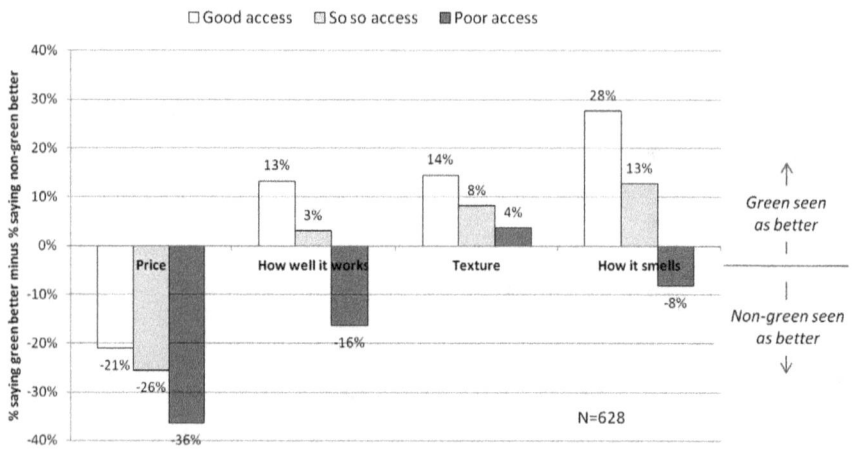

SWIMMING AGAINST THE
CLIMATE CHANGE TIDE

I t has been well documented that an increasingly vocal minority
of Americans (British too according to a recent *New York Times*
article) think that the threat of climate change is overblown,
nonexistent, or at the very least, not manmade. Then you have
the many Americans that believe climate change is happening
at an alarming rate, and in the middle are those who think it is
happening but who are not that worried about it.

It appears that lately the arguments of skeptics have been winning
new believers as Naomi Oreskes and Erik M. Conway describe in
the blog *Yale environment 360:*

> *In recent months, as the U.S. Senate prepared to consider climate
> and energy legislation, there has been a stepped-up effort on a broad
> front to belittle the overwhelming evidence of human-caused global
> warming...In the case of global warming, there is strong evidence*

that this contrarian campaign is enjoying success, with recent polls showing that more than half of Americans are not particularly worried about the issue and that fully 40 percent believe there is major disagreement among scientists about whether climate change is even occurring.

Still, things have to be kept in perspective. Green Meridian's study *Sustainability in the Mainstream* study found that only 9% of women solidly agreed (i.e., 6 or 7 rating on 1-7 scale) with the statement, "Global warming is *not* really a problem." And another 6% mildly agreed with it. Not exactly an avalanche of doubt about global warming. In addition, a more recent survey by the Political Psychology Research Group found that "huge majorities of Americans still believe the earth has been gradually warming as the result of human activity and want the government to institute regulations to stop it."

Should green marketers be concerned about climate change skepticism?

Perhaps. But climate change **apathy** poses an even greater threat to green marketing efforts than climate change **skepticism**. The *Sustainability in the Mainstream* study shows that consumers that believe we have serious environmental problems *and who are worried about them* are more likely *to want to buy green*. Note two things:

- <u>Give me your worried</u>: The study shows that believing, by itself, that environmental problems are serious is not usually enough to motivate women to buy green. They also have to be worried about the problems.

- <u>Wanting to be green is not the same as actually being green but it's a start</u>: I said "*want to* buy green" rather than just "buy green" since there are many women that want to buy green but haven't yet for several reasons (e.g., high price, poor brand awareness, etc.) that have nothing to do with their levels of concern about products' environmental impacts.

Can green marketers do anything about eco-apathy?

Yes. First, companies can fund programs that educate the public about climate change as Hewlett-Packard did with the National Environmental Education Week.

More immediately, green marketers should segment consumers on their attitudes towards climate change and other environmental issues since receptivity to green products is tied to consumers' eco-attitudes even if products' greenness is often a secondary driver of purchase decisions. A secondary driver can still be a tiebreaker, though, all other things being equal.

As I said before, both a *belief* in the seriousness of global warming and other environmental problems combined with a substantial *level of engagement* with environmental issues (i.e., they're worried too) predisposes a consumer to be more motivated to buy green. This approach allows us to identify the *Worriers*, who are the best targets for green marketers. The diagram below shows a simple scheme to segment consumers using these two attitudinal dimensions.

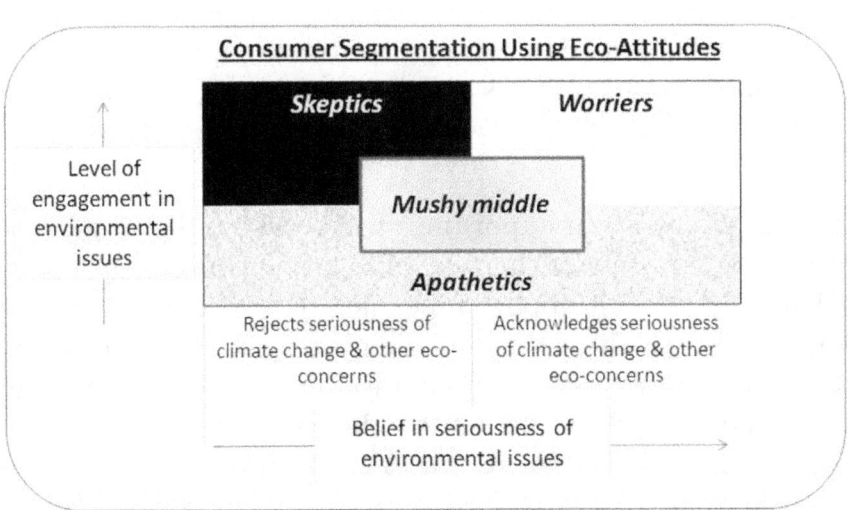

Have segmentation, will target and message

Thinking about consumers in terms of both their beliefs and their level of environmental concern provides a valuable framework for developing appropriate targeting and messaging approaches. Let's look at each segment:

Skeptics: A product that touts its greenness may tick off these folks. As Erich Schwartzel of the Pittsburgh Post-Gazette said, "Not everyone's going to love it when a company goes green."

- Recommendation: I wouldn't blow the bank marketing to skeptics. Unless your green claims play a small role in your product's messaging, be very leery of devoting too many resources to this group.

Apathetics: Whether they believe global warming and other environmental issues are serious is irrelevant. This group focuses almost exclusively on conventional product features and if you can offer superiority on these, then *Apathetics* will flock to your product.

- Recommendation: Evaluate how compelling the story about your product's more conventional features is. If it's strong enough, *Apathetics* may be receptive to hearing it.

Worriers: Much of your opportunity will be with this group but you have to be clear about the type of consumer in this group with which your greatest opportunities lie. *Worriers* are not homogenous. There are those that walk their worried talk by buying and living green and those who do not for a variety of reasons. If you can effectively address the reasons that prevent some consumers from turning their eco-worries into green purchases – most commonly high price as well as low green brand awareness and availability – then the latter subgroup should also be a target for your green brand. And for almost all *Worriers*, remember that you still

need to offer appealing product features beyond eco-friendliness (i.e., it better work well and not cost an arm and a leg).

- Recommendation: Figure out whether your product is better suited for the *Worriers* already buying green or those who would like to buy more green (or both subgroups). With the already green, you need to build a rationale for why your green product is preferable to other green products. For the *Green Aspirants* that want to green their buying but have been unable to, you have to first understand the barriers preventing them from buying green and find ways to surmount these barriers.

The Mushy Middle: In the *Sustainability in the Mainstream* study, 53% of women rated their level of agreement with the statement "I think the planet is in very poor shape" 3 to 5 on a 1 to 7 scale. The slightly more subdued statement, "Global warming is not really a problem" had 32% of women rating their agreement with it a lukewarm 3 to 5. Despite the passionate talk of pundits on both sides of the issue, as marketers **we need to remember that many Americans are actually somewhere in the middle**. Many may believe global warming is real and manmade but that doesn't mean that it is one of the chief concerns in their daily lives.

- Recommendation: If you decide to target them, approach the *Mushy Middle* basically as you would the *Apathetics* but add a dash of environmental messaging. The *MMs* may not be that worried but they do believe that something's not right with the environment.

The bottom line
I wouldn't let climate change skeptics affect your green marketing campaign since the rock solid skeptics are relatively few in number and it would be a huge uphill battle to neutralize and

then convert their negative perceptions of your green product. As far as apathetic consumers and the so-called *Mushy Middle*, you first have to decide whether they should be targeted and if they should, what non-environmental story you're going to tell them about your product. Finally, you must decide whether to just target worriers that have *already gone green* or also those who *haven't yet* but *want to*. Thinking in terms of "eco-attitude" segments prevents you from wasting valuable promotional resources on the wrong consumers and helps you fine-tune your message to each group's eco-attitudes.

II

UNCONVENTIONAL WISDOM

GREEN CRED AND THE BRAND MANAGER'S TO-DO LIST

Making credible product claims is not a *nice-to-do* for marketers, be they green or not, but a *have-to-do*. You can make compelling claims that distinguish your product from competitors but if no one believes them, game over. Not only can making phony claims get a marketer into hot water with consumers but with regulators as well.

Recently, green product claims have been monitored especially closely by watchdogs such as the Greenwashing Index, the federal government, retailers like Walmart, and third party rating services like GoodGuide. Many involved in green marketing believe that consumers' distrust of green claims is a key force holding many green products back from mass market acceptance.

Bikini season for corporate America

With the increased scrutiny of companies' environmental and other practices, books like *The Naked Corporation* advise, "if you have to be naked, you had better be buff." And companies are hard at work making themselves and their products buff, particularly in the environmental arena. Seminars to help companies avoid being charged with greenwashing have proliferated. In addition, rather than ignoring ratings firms like GoodGuide, companies work with such firms to ensure that their products don't receive failing grades. Finally, attorneys and green marketing consultants help green marketers develop environmental claims that won't lead to legal and market blowback.

So much to do

How should the manager of a green brand deal with this intense scrutiny? First, let's take a step back and think about all the different goals a green brand manager has. As the brand manager drafts his marketing plan for the coming year, he is thinking about how he's going to:

1. Build brand awareness

2. Create positive perceptions of the brand on features having nothing to do with its environmental footprint (e.g., price, quality, availability in stores, smell, texture, fairly traded, etc.)

3. Create positive perceptions of the brand on green-related features (e.g., environmental impact, healthfulness)

4. Induce product trial and encourage repeat purchase

In short, the green marketer has to allocate his budget, not to mention his time, across a variety of objectives with objective #3, creating positive green perceptions of the brand, being just one of them. In addition, in terms of importance, one could argue that objective #3 may even lag the other ones. Why?

- <u>Consumers may not even be paying attention to your brand</u>: First, if consumers aren't aware of your brand, nothing else you do will matter. And Green Meridian's *Sustainability in the Mainstream* study shows that many green household cleaner and personal care product brands have a **big awareness problem**. [See Data Deep Dives #10 and & 11 for more details.]

- <u>Greenness is a less important product feature</u>: For most consumers, even the greenest ones, products' price and quality typically play greater roles in consumers' purchasing decisions than products' greenness. And for many less green consumers, the greenness of a product is a **non-factor** in purchase decisions. *Sustainability in the Mainstream* found that although some women are skeptical of products' green claims, this distrust pales in importance when compared with poor perceptions of green products' price, availability, and quality as barriers to green product purchase. [See Data Deep Dives #2, 6, 7 & 12 for more details.]

Credential fatigue

Green credibility is very useful as a defensive strategy to prevent the harsh glare of the consumers', activists', and regulatory spotlights from spotlighting any warts. However, going beyond that and attempting to distinguish a green product with an impressive list of eco-credentials will yield diminishing returns when compared with all the other activities a brand manager needs to be doing to promote his product.

So where should efforts to develop green cred sit on a brand manager's to-do list? If it's considered the Holy Grail and resourced as such, then other crucial promotional activities will suffer. However, green cred efforts should be a key part of a balanced marketing program that contains several other more traditional marketing activities that are at least as important for sustainable products' success.

Data Deep Dive #10

Percentage of Women Aware of Green Household Cleaner Brands (Unaided)

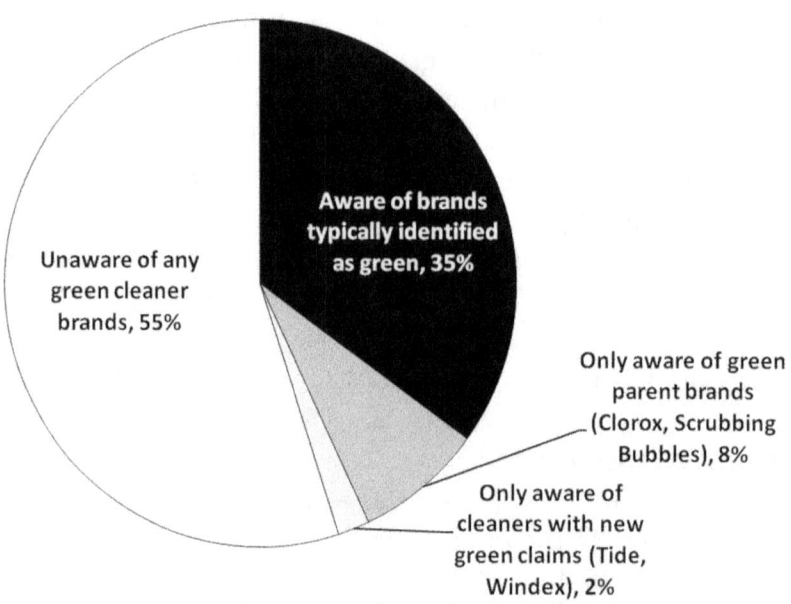

 **Data Deep Dive #11**

Percentage of Women Aware of Green Personal Care Brands (Unaided)

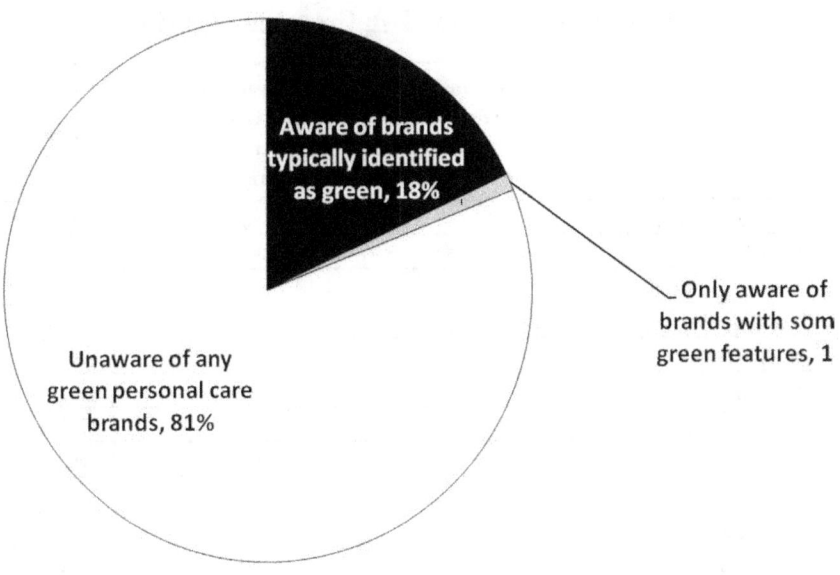

Aware of brands typically identified as green, 18%

Only aware of brands with som green features, 1

Unaware of any green personal care brands, 81%

Data Deep Dive #12

Perceptions of Green vs. Non-Green
Personal Care Products

Perceptions of Green vs. Non-Green Household Cleaners			
N=628	**% Considering Green Products Better (6 or 7 ratings*)**	**% Considering Non-Green Products Better (1 or 2 ratings*)**	**Difference**
Effect on environment	58%	6%	52%
Healthfulness	55%	6%	49%
Company's values	35%	6%	29%
Treatment of workers	25%	5%	20%
Perceived status	24%	9%	14%
How it smells	27%	13%	14%
Country where made	20%	7%	13%
Texture	17%	9%	8%
Recommendations	16%	13%	3%
Advertising	12%	13%	-1%
How well it works	18%	20%	-2%
Availability	15%	28%	-13%
Price	16%	38%	-22%

*On a 1-7 scale.

LIMOUSINE LIBERALS

One of the hoariest stereotypes is that of the conservative voter who believes global warming is a hoax and who drives a big gas guzzling vehicle. And, on the other side, is the liberal that is ultra-concerned about the environment and who tools around in her Prius with the Save the Whales bumper sticker. A recent study by Green Meridian that looked at the green purchasing (of household cleaners and personal care products) as well as the underlying attitudes of over 600 women suggests that while certain facts support these stereotypes, many do not.

First let's be clear about political labels. The study found that many more women identify themselves as middle-of-the-road (25%) or independent (29%) than either conservative (19%) or liberal (14%). While the Green Meridian survey does not capture which way the independent and the middle-of the-road folks each lean, there are still some interesting learnings to be gained from looking at the political affiliation data.

Holy Boulder, what's going on?
One would think that people that label themselves liberals are the greenest of the green in terms of what they buy and how they think about the environment. And self-proclaimed conservatives would be at the other end of the spectrum. Sorry, not really.

Green Meridian actually found that *similar* proportions of conservative and liberal women are *Frequent Greens*, those women that buy green household cleaners and personal care products the greatest percentage of the time. Political middle-of-the-roaders buy like conservatives and liberals do. The green purchasing champs, albeit by a moderate amount, are those women calling themselves political independents. The apathetic women that say "don't know/don't care" when asked their political affiliations are the least green. [See Data Deep Dive #13 for more details.]

I don't want to totally rock everyone's world though. There is a finding that does conform to our stereotypes of liberals and conservatives. Although proportionally similar numbers of conservatives and liberals are *Frequent Greens*, a greater percentage of the *remaining* (i.e., not yet green) liberal women aspire to be greener than their conservative peers. However, in terms of aspirations to green up, middle-of-the-roaders and independents (yet again) have both conservatives and liberals beat. The politically apathetic women also tend to be apathetic about becoming more green, similar to conservative women. [See Data Deep Dive #14 for more details.]

It's those women that resist political labels rather than self-styled liberals who are green marketers' best friends.

But liberals worry more about the environment, right?
Again, the liberal vs. conservative comparison yields a mixed bag. Liberals, like middle-of-the-road women and independents, are

more likely than conservatives and politically apathetic women to acknowledge that we're facing serious environmental problems. However, the difference between conservatives and liberals narrows on *how worried* about the environment each group is. In terms of feelings of responsibility for the environment, liberals and conservatives are about the same with independents and middle-of-the-roaders actually feeling more responsible. Finally, true to stereotypes about the Religious Right, conservatives are much more likely than the other groups (41% of conservatives vs. 27% of women overall) to agree that their religion teaches them that we need to be stewards of the earth. Confused?

Not to pile on liberals, but the *Wall Street Journal* also recently took a whack at stereotypes about liberals. It appears that Boulder's city government is having a tough time changing the earth-unfriendly behaviors of many of the city's legendarily liberal citizens. Old behaviors die hard even for dyed in the sustainable wool liberals.

So are these stereotype busters good for green marketers?

No and Yes. **No**, because unpredictability makes targeting tougher. Green marketers cannot automatically assume that the traditional liberal precincts are going to automatically be where their best targets live.

Political independents (and to some extent middle of the road women) should be a group of great interest to green marketers. They certainly are to prognosticators of presidential race outcomes. To add to marketers' targeting challenges, independents and middle-of-the-roaders are not the easiest to demographically define. The Green Meridian study shows them to be similar in demographics to the nation as a whole. And the definition of a political independent, like the definition of a green product, can be nebulous and variable.

Perhaps dividing these groups further by political leaning would clear things up a bit. Given what we've learned about conservatives and liberals, though, we shouldn't be too certain.

And now for a reason to rejoice: **Yes**, green marketers should be happy that opportunities in the mainstream abound and the most successful marketers will figure out how to reach those **green-receptive consumers that exist across a variety of geographies, political orientations, ethnicities, educational levels, and incomes**. Green marketers need not fight a battle to the death with each other for a relatively limited number of green consumers confined to the Boulder's, Berkeley's, and Burlington's. The successful green marketer will be the one that looks well beyond the archetypal liberal enclaves.

 # Data Deep Dive #13

Political Orientation of Green Purchasing Groups

Political orientation	Total Population (n=628)	Non-Greens (n=301)	Moderate Greens (n=191)	Frequent Greens (n=136)
		A	B	C
Conservative	19.3%	20.0%ₐ	15.7%ₐ	22.8%ₐ
Liberal	14.5%	15.0%ₐ	15.1%ₐ	12.6%ₐ
Middle-of-the-road	25.1%	25.4%ₐ	24.8%ₐ	24.8%ₐ
Independent, depends on the issue	29.4%	22.1%ₐ	35.8%ᵦ	36.5%ᵦ
Don't know / don't care	11.7%	17.5%ₐ	8.6%ᵦ	3.3%ᵦ
	100.0%	100.0%	100.0%	100.0%

Results are based on two-sided tests with significance level 0.05. For each significant pair, the key of the category with the smaller column proportion appears under the category with the larger column proportion. Tests are adjusted for all pairwise comparisons within a row of each innermost subtable using the Bonferroni correction.

Data Deep Dive #14

Political Orientation of Green Intention Groups

Political orientation	Total Population (n= 628)	Status Quo's (n=332)	Green Aspirants (n=160)	Frequent Greens (n=136)
		A	B	C
Conservative	19.3%	20.9%$_a$	12.9%$_a$	22.8%$_a$
Liberal	14.5%	15.6%$_a$	13.9%$_a$	12.6%$_a$
Middle-of-the-road	25.1%	24.4%$_a$	26.9%$_a$	24.8%$_a$
Independent, depends on the issue	29.4%	23.2%$_a$	36.1%$_b$	36.5%$_b$
Don't know / don't care	11.7%	15.9%$_a$	10.3%$_{a,b}$	3.3%$_b$
	100.0%	100.0%	100.0%	100.0%

Results are based on two-sided tests with significance level 0.05. For each significant pair, the key of the category with the smaller column proportion appears under the category with the larger column proportion. Tests are adjusted for all pairwise comparisons within a row of each innermost subtable using the Bonferroni correction.

GO EASY ON THE TWEETS

Facebook, Twitter, and other social media are undeniably becoming increasingly important to marketers as more and more people spend great chunks of time communicating via them. For green marketers, it may seem particularly natural to target the ostensibly sophisticated, hip upscale green consumer through these media.

While social media should be an important part of the green marketing mix, data from **Green Meridian's** *Sustainability in the Mainstream* study raises a yellow flag of caution about overreliance on it.

When asked what their favorite ways to learn about green products were, various types of social media were pretty far down the list of information sources preferred by women including those women that most frequently purchase green products, the so-called *Frequent Greens.*

Women's Preferred Sources of Information on Green Products

% agreeing	Total Population (n=628)	Non-Greens (n=301)	Moderate Greens (n=191)	Frequent Greens (n=136)
Information source		A	B	C
Magazines that rate products	**41.5%**	$34.9\%_a$	$43.4\%_{a,b}$	$53.4\%_b$
Product labels and other co. info.	**40.9%**	$28.6\%_a$	$46.6\%_b$	$60.5\%_c$
Opinions of scientists/other experts	**35.0%**	$25.3\%_a$	$39.2\%_b$	$50.6\%_b$
Ratings by other consumers	**31.5%**	$27.3\%_a$	$30.7\%_{a,b}$	$41.9\%_b$
Magazine or newspaper article	**30.7%**	$23.4\%_a$	$31.6\%_a$	$45.7\%_b$
Green product advertising	**28.4%**	$15.8\%_a$	$34.9\%_b$	$47.0\%_b$
School or continuing ed. programs	**26.1%**	$18.4\%_a$	$27.9\%_b$	$40.8\%_c$
Television show	**25.9%**	$20.3\%_a$	$26.6\%_{a,b}$	$37.3\%_b$
Friends	**25.4%**	$17.8\%_a$	$25.8\%_a$	$41.8\%_b$
Husband or partner (n=322)	**24.2%**	$21.7\%_a$	$21.8\%_a$	$32.7\%_a$
National environmental groups	**19.8%**	$14.0\%_a$	$18.1\%_a$	$35.3\%_b$
Other relatives	**17.1%**	$14.0\%_a$	$16.7\%_{a,b}$	$24.5\%_b$
Books / books on CD	**13.8%**	$8.7\%_a$	$10.6\%_a$	$29.9\%_b$
Children (n=316)	**13.3%**	$5.5\%_a$	$15.0\%_b$	$30.4\%_c$
Store salespeople	**12.9%**	$6.7\%_a$	$14.8\%_b$	$23.8\%_b$
Online discussion groups for moms	**12.8%**	$7.9\%_a$	$12.2\%_a$	$24.5\%_b$
Community groups	**12.3%**	$8.2\%_a$	$10.2\%_a$	$24.3\%_b$
General online discussion groups	**11.8%**	$6.5\%_a$	$15.7\%_b$	$18.2\%_b$
Blogs by other women	**10.9%**	$4.7\%_a$	$12.2\%_b$	$22.8\%_c$
Radio show	**9.9%**	$4.2\%_a$	$9.9\%_b$	$22.5\%_c$
Facebook	**9.3%**	$5.6\%_a$	$8.6\%_a$	$18.6\%_b$
Blogs by men	**6.6%**	$3.4\%_a$	$8.0\%_{a,b}$	$11.9\%_b$
MySpace	**5.2%**	$2.1\%_a$	$5.2\%_{a,b}$	$12.1\%_b$
Twitter	**5.1%**	$1.8\%_a$	$6.3\%_b$	$11.0\%_b$

Such old school information sources as *Consumer Reports*, product labels, and advertising trumped blogs, Facebook, and Twitter in importance. Less green women reported that they relied on social media even less than their greener brethren for information about green products.

Indeed, marketers such as Marc Brownstein, president of Philadelphia ad agency Brownstein Group, warn against transferring all or most of a brand's ad spending to social media. He asks, "How will customers find you? Why should they care about your product/service? What are you going to do when your competitors crank up their promotional spend and start taking your customers? This message is simple — the short-term delight of not spending any media dollars on advertising will surely have a long-term effect: brand erosion." ("Overreliance on Social Media Will Damage Your Brand", *Advertising Age*, May 10, 2010)

Don't give up on social media though

However, while it doesn't make sense to bet the house on social media that doesn't mean that social media are without value. Other data from the *Sustainability in the Mainstream* study suggests that women understate the role recommendations and, by extension, social media (e.g., the increasing visibility of friends' recommendations on Facebook) play in their purchasing of household cleaners and personal care products.

We see a pretty strong relationship between the amount of green cleaners and personal care products women buy and the degree to which their friends and others recommend green products vs. non-green ones. It is also quite likely that women's cleaner and personal care specific *brand choices* are influenced by recommendations.

We may think we're independent, logical arbiters of what products best meet our needs but the reality is we often depend on a little help from our friends (and families and neighbors). Green marketers need to leverage consumers' social networks, which social media have vastly expanded, to get the word out about their products. Just make sure not to forget about more traditional promotional channels in the process.

III

SPARKING & HARNESSING ECO-CONCERNS

TAKE A HIKE

One would think that those women that often buy green household cleaners and personal care products would be able to rattle off a long list of facts and figures about the environment. Surprise! While not being a definitive test of eco-knowledge, six true/false factual questions asked of respondents to a survey fielded by Green Meridian yielded statistically similar results for the greenest women compared with those that are least green (table below).

Frequent Greens' Unimpressive Eco-Knowledge

Statement	% *least* green women answering correctly (n=249)	% *most* green women answering correctly (n=136)
Plugged in appliances can still use energy even when they're turned off.	92%	92%
The US produces about 25% of the gases that contribute to global warming.	80%	82%
Oil and gas are considered renewable resources.	58%	67%
In the US, burning coal adds to global warming more than anything else Americans do.	38%	47%
In the US, the biggest contributor to global warming is driving cars.	33%	31%
Some of the aerosol cans in stores contain chloroflurocarbons, which can hurt the ozone layer.	10%	10%

These results tentatively suggest that a strong knowledge of cold, hard facts about the environment is not automatically going to make someone hardcore green. Conversely, ignorance of the facts should not be seen as a deal killer. Thus, the oft-heard lament, "If only people were more educated about the environment," while a noble sentiment, may have less relevance to green product success than is commonly thought.

Nature lovers, not eco-geniuses, wanted

A consumer taking a hike probably has more value to a green marketer than one reading the latest book or article about our warming planet. *80%* of women that are frequent green shoppers (*Frequent Greens*) surveyed by Green Meridian reported spending some or a lot of time doing activities in nature compared with only *39%* of the least green women. In fact, 85% of *Frequent Greens* cited the desire to preserve nature so they can continue to enjoy it as a reason for them to purchase green products. [See Data Deep Dives #15 & #16 for more details.]

So green marketers should have two goals:

1. First, get the couch potatoes to go outside even if it means they have to take a break from watching a documentary on global warming.

2. Then show how using your products can benefit the outdoor spaces where consumers like to play. Doing this will connect green products to a spot that is a rung or two down from several powerful emotional benefits on the traditional product benefits ladder marketers use to position brands.

 **Data Deep Dive #15**

Amount of Time Spent Doing Nature Activities by Green Purchasing Groups

	Total Population (n=628)	Non-Green's (n=301)	Moderate Greens (n=191)	Frequent Greens (n=136)
Amount of time spent doing activities in nature		A	B	C
No time	10.7%	17.2%$_a$	4.3%$_b$	5.0%$_b$
Little time	31.8%	43.2%$_a$	25.8%$_b$	15.1%$_b$
Some time	44.7%	33.9%$_a$	55.1%$_b$	54.1%$_b$
A lot of time	12.8%	5.6%$_a$	14.8%$_b$	25.9%$_c$
	100.0%	100.0%	100.0%	100.0%

Results are based on two-sided tests with significance level 0.05. For each significant pair, the key of the category with the smaller column proportion appears under the category with the larger column proportion. Tests are adjusted for all pairwise comparisons within a row of each innermost subtable using the Bonferroni correction.

Data Deep Dive #16

Drivers of Green Product Use among Green Purchasing Groups

% seeing as a driver	Total Population (n=576)	Non-Greens (n=249)	Moderate Greens (n=191)	Frequent Greens (n=136)
		A	B	C
Green products are healthier for my family and me.	70.5%	58.7%ₐ	71.4%ᵦ	91.1%ᵧ
I am concerned about what we're leaving to future generations.	65.0%	50.9%ₐ	69.4%ᵦ	84.8%ᵧ
I want to help preserve nature so that I can continue to enjoy it.	63.9%	48.7%ₐ	68.4%ᵦ	85.4%ᵧ
I want to help the planet.	61.2%	43.7%ₐ	71.6%ᵦ	78.8%ᵦ
I want to help my community's environment.	55.6%	39.0%ₐ	65.2%ᵦ	72.7%ᵦ
Green household cleaners and personal care products are available where I shop.	51.9%	42.4%ₐ	54.5%ᵦ	65.6%ᵦ
I want to feel like I have some say in the direction in which this planet's headed.	49.6%	35.7%ₐ	54.6%ᵦ	68.1%ᵧ
It makes me feel like a good person.	48.4%	36.5%ₐ	53.0%ᵦ	63.7%ᵦ
I want to live more simply.	47.0%	31.8%ₐ	50.1%ᵦ	70.7%ᵧ
Green household cleaners and personal care products work better than the non-green ones.	38.0%	36.6%ₐ	36.0%ₐ	43.5%ₐ
The green products are cheaper.	33.7%	36.9%ₐ	32.9%ₐ	29.0%ₐ
I like the companies that make the green products I've bought.	33.4%	21.4%ₐ	34.6%ᵦ	53.6%ᵧ
The green products smell better.	32.1%	23.8%ₐ	32.3%ₐ	47.4%ᵦ
It makes me feel less guilty.	32.1%	22.0%ₐ	35.0%ᵦ	46.9%ᵦ
Friends or other family members recommended them.	25.0%	16.2%ₐ	24.4%ₐ	42.2%ᵦ
My spouse, partner, or someone else in the household asked me to buy green.	22.4%	16.0%ₐ	21.4%ₐ	35.6%ᵦ
Many celebrities buy green products.	10.3%	6.2%ₐ	8.2%ₐ	20.9%ᵦ

Results are based on two-sided tests with significance level 0.05. For each significant pair, the key of the category with the smaller column proportion appears under the category with the larger column proportion. Tests are adjusted for all pairwise comparisons within a row of each innermost subtable using the Bonferroni correction.

WILL ANY IN THE MAINSTREAM BUY GREEN TO SAVE THE EARTH?

Most analysts agree that there's a core of green consumers whose ecological concerns are central to their world view and these concerns are reflected in their purchases. Green Meridian's study *Sustainability in the Mainstream* identified a group of such consumers, dubbed *Frequent Greens* that represent about one-fifth of women.

What about the other four-fifths of women, which I'll call "the mainstream" for simplicity's sake? How often do they think about a product's environmental impact when they make a purchase? The answer is "not very often." Only about 15% of these women say they think about a household cleaner's environmental impact all or almost all of the time when making a purchase (17% for personal care products). By contrast, 62% of the greenest women think about a household cleaner's eco-impact all or almost all the time (63% for personal care products). [See Data Deep Dives #1, 3A, and 3B for more details.]

At this point, you might be thinking: "Yeah I get it. If we're going to get the mainstream to buy green it won't be out of any concern for the planet." As Jacquie Ottman advised in a post to her *Green Marketing Blog,* "to appeal to the mainstream, green products must appeal to more than just a consumer's eco-conscience. It must appeal in some way to their self-interest [i.e., health]."

Are most mainstream women that wrapped up in everyday concerns that the condition of the planet is often an afterthought, as Joel Makower suggests in his book *Strategies for the Green Economy?* Makower says, "For most folks, *saving the planet* usually takes a back seat to *saving the day.*" I agree but I would add that even though saving the planet may be taking a backseat, for some mainstream women environmental concerns are *still in the car and that's significant to green marketers.*

Meet the mainstream's *Green Aspirants*
One-third of the mainstream say they would like to buy more green household cleaners and personal care products but have been unable to so far and we've called this group *Green Aspirants.* Like their *Frequent Green* peers, many *Green Aspirants* (59% of them) are very worried about the shape of the environment and they are just as likely as *Frequent Greens* to strongly believe they can help the environment by buying green products. [See Data Deep Dives #17 and #18 for more details.]

So far so good. So where are *Green Aspirants* veering off the path to becoming *Frequent Greens?* The answer is with obstacles that have nothing to do with a product's greenness, such as the perceived high cost of green products, their poor availability, and to some extent, a feeling that green products are of lower quality than non-green ones.

On the positive side for green household cleaners, somewhat more *Green Aspirants* than not see green cleaners as being superior on smell to non-green ones. And a cleaner's smell factors very often into women's cleaner purchasing decisions. Not surprisingly, green cleaners' lower environmental impact and greater product healthfulness were also cited as green product strengths by *Green Aspirants*. [See Data Deep Dive #19 for more details.]

So what's the problem? The problem lies in the relative importance of different product features used by these women in choosing a cleaner. Product healthfulness, which frequently figures into the cleaner purchase deliberations of over half the *Green Aspirants*, still lags product price and effectiveness in importance. And what about the environmental impact of household cleaners? Only a quarter of *Green Aspirants* say they often think about a cleaner's environmental impact when making a cleaner purchase (vs. 62% of *Frequent Greens*). [See Data Deep Dive #20 for more details.]

So why talk about environment at all with *Green Aspirants?*

A green marketer's logical take away from this data would be: "I'm going to first work on improving *Green Aspirants'* perceptions of the non-green features of my product. Then, when I talk about my product's greenness with these women, I'm going to focus more on how my product is healthier than on how the product helps the planet. These women say they're worried about the environment but it doesn't matter if that concern can't be translated into action."

That would be the most logical explanation and it may be right. Let's just consider, though, an alternative possibility. First, many people would agree that sustainable products are often not in *Green Aspirants'* consideration set because of the high cost, poor availability, and sometimes inferior quality with which GA's perceive green products. So if the only products offering an environmental benefit are often not an option for *Green Aspirants,* then environmental impact often doesn't even have a chance to be at the table of purchase factors.

So why is a product's healthfulness considered fairly frequently by these women? Because healthfulness is not a feature exclusive to green products. For instance, a disinfectant can lay claim to being healthy for the household while few people would call most disinfectants green. *Green Aspirants* thus have more opportunities to consider products' relative healthfulness than their environmental impact.

When to trumpet eco-friendly features to *Green Aspirants*

However, even if green products were more accessible to *Green Aspirants,* I still think products' environmental impacts would be trumped by several other product features in terms of relative importance in consumer decision making. **But if parity or near-parity is achieved on key product features, I would argue that you will see the importance of products' environmental impact shoot up dramatically for *Green Aspirants*.** They care. They're worried. But they currently see the barriers to buying green as often outweighing the benefits. Tear down these barriers and now you can talk climate change and overflowing landfills with the *Aspirants.*

So, to sum up, I don't think consumers neatly split into green and non-green groups. There's a light green-tinged group in the mainstream that will likely buy more green products to help the environment and their families' health when the barriers to buying green are lowered.

What do you think? Am I reaching for tendencies in these shoppers that aren't there?

Data Deep Dive #17

General Environmental Attitudes of Green Intention Groups

% agreeing	Total Population (n= 628)	Status Quo's (n=332)	Green Aspirants (n=160)	Frequent Greens (n=136)
Attitudinal statement		A	B	C
Americans' desire for more "things," such as SUVs and big screen TVs, has hurt the environment.	43.3%	29.7%ₐ	57.6%♭	59.8%♭
I am worried about the shape of our environment.	40.3%	22.9%ₐ	59.3%♭	60.5%♭
I think our planet is in very poor shape.	33.7%	23.2%ₐ	44.2%♭	47.2%♭
Global warming is not really a problem.	8.9%	9.5%ₐ	5.1%ₐ	12.1%ₐ
The condition of the environment doesn't really affect my family and me.	7.7%	7.3%ₐ	8.9%ₐ	7.4%ₐ

Results are based on two-sided tests with significance level 0.05. For each significant pair, the key of the category with the smaller column proportion appears under the category with the larger column proportion. Tests are adjusted for all pairwise comparisons within a row of each innermost subtable using the Bonferroni correction.

Data Deep Dive #18

Personal Approach to Being Green of Green
Intention Groups

% agreeing	Total Population (n= 628)	Status Quo's (n=332)	Green Aspirants (n=160)	Frequent Greens (n=136)
Attitudinal statement		A	B	C
I can really help the environment by buying green products.	39.2%	22.5%ₐ	61.2%♭	54.1%♭
I will try harder to be green once this recession is over.	23.0%	9.6%ₐ	38.6%♭	37.2%♭
I have to make big sacrifices to buy mainly green products.	20.9%	17.7%ₐ	30.6%♭	17.4%ₐ
I'm too busy dealing with other things to really get into the whole green thing.	17.9%	24.0%ₐ	13.2%♭	8.7%♭
I am very open to paying more if a product is better for the environment.	14.5%	5.8%ₐ	17.0%♭	32.6%𝒸
Making sure the environment is in good shape is not my job.	7.5%	5.2%ₐ	3.8%ₐ	17.4%♭

Results are based on two-sided tests with significance level 0.05. For each significant pair, the key of the category with the smaller column proportion appears under the category with the larger column proportion. Tests are adjusted for all pairwise comparisons within a row of each innermost subtable using the Bonferroni correction.

Data Deep Dive #19

Ratings of Green vs. Non-Green Personal Care Products by Green Intention Groups

N=628	Status Quo's (n=332)		Green Aspirants (n=160)		Frequent Greens (n=136)	
	%Considering Green Products Better (6,7)	%Considering Non-Green Products Better (1,2)	%Considering Green Products Better (6,7)	%Considering Non-Green Products Better (1,2)	%Considering Green Products Better (6,7)	%Considering Non-Green Products Better (1,2)
How making and using the product affect the environment[F]	40%	7%	71%	4%	78%	3%
How good product is for the health of me and my family[GF]	37%	7%	65%	6%	81%	3%
Company's values, ethics, principles[F]	18%	8%	36%	5%	49%	3%
How the company that makes the product treats workers involved in manufacturing it	13%	6%	28%	5%	48%	2%
How it smells[SGF]	14%	15%	24%	17%	49%	9%
Country where made[F]	8%	9%	23%	6%	36%	7%
Whether product is considered high status	17%	12%	26%	9%	22%	12%
Texture / how it feels[GF]	9%	13%	19%	10%	41%	5%
Recommendations from friends and family	7%	17%	24%	9%	34%	5%
How well it works[SGF]	13%	22%	24%	22%	43%	11%
Products' advertising	5%	19%	14%	22%	19%	10%
How available product is in the stores where I shop[SGF]	9%	32%	20%	35%	27%	22%
Price[SGF]	14%	43%	15%	42%	27%	22%

Data Deep Dive #20

% of Each Green Intention Group Saying
Cleaner Feature is Important

	Total Population (n= 628)	Status Quo's (n=332)	Green Aspirants (n=160)	Frequent Greens (n=136)
		A	B	C
How well it works	86.5%	83.9%$_a$	89.6%$_a$	89.3%$_a$
Price	77.6%	78.0%$_a$	79.7%$_a$	74.0%$_a$
How it smells	61.6%	55.2%$_a$	71.9%$_b$	65.0%$_{a,b}$
How available product is in the stores where I shop	52.5%	46.8%$_a$	59.3%$_b$	58.6%$_{a,b}$
How good product is for the health of me and my family	49.5%	34.2%$_a$	55.6%$_b$	79.9%$_c$
Texture / how it feels	32.3%	20.7%$_a$	42.6%$_b$	48.6%$_b$
Country where it was made	26.1%	13.5%$_a$	31.6%$_b$	50.6%$_c$
Recommendations from friends, family	26.0%	20.3%$_a$	29.0%$_{a,b}$	36.2%$_b$
How making and using the product affect the environment	24.3%	8.6%$_a$	25.5%$_b$	61.6%$_c$
Company's values, ethics, principles	21.1%	9.5%$_a$	23.2%$_b$	47.0%$_c$
How the company that makes the product treats workers involved in manufacturing it	18.5%	9.5%$_a$	18.6%$_b$	40.2%$_c$
Whether product is considered high status	12.8%	6.5%$_a$	14.9%$_b$	25.6%$_b$
Product's advertising	12.1%	8.9%$_a$	14.1%$_{a,b}$	17.4%$_b$

Results are based on two-sided tests with significance level 0.05. For each significant pair, the key of the category with the smaller column proportion appears under the category with the larger column proportion. Tests are adjusted for all pairwise comparisons within a row of each innermost subtable using the Bonferroni correction

More on Sleeper Greens in the Mainstream

There are women in the mainstream (i.e., defined as those women making green cleaner purchases less than half the time) that are **primed to increase their green purchasing if the conditions are right**. They represent a significant opportunity to green cleaner marketers because:

- There's a lot of room to grow their green cleaner usage from current modest levels.

- These women **want** to green their cleaner and personal care purchases.

These so-called *Green Aspirants* were one of four segments Green Meridian identified in its marketing research study, *Sustainability in the Mainstream that* we fielded with over 650 women at the end of 2009.

So why, among the four segments, did *Green Aspirants* especially catch our eye? In short, because they are **most in flux** and that spells **opportunity for marketers**. With *Green Aspirants*, green product marketers have the chance to grab customers who currently buy modest amounts of green cleaners and personal care products but who want to change that. With the other customer segments, it's more a battle between brands than one between "brown" and green products. But with *Green Aspirants*, it's **Green Brands vs. Brown Brands**, which presents a valuable opportunity to tell the story about the green benefits of your products be they ecological or health-oriented.

What's more, if we look at the future green cleaner purchasing levels women predict for themselves, we see that *Green Aspirants* may account for **half the growth of green cleaner purchasing** in the future although only 25% of women are *Green Aspirants*.

Who are the *Green Aspirants?*

- More likely to be middle-aged (45-54) and less likely to be older (55+).

- Tend to live more frequently in the West & Midwest and less frequently in the South.

- More likely to be married and single and less likely to be divorced or widowed.

- More Latina and Asian-American tinged than the overall population.

[See Data Deep Dive #21 for more details.]

How do we know *Green Aspirants* are primed to buy more green cleaners?

- <u>They say so</u>: They agree with the statement, *"I'd like to buy more green household cleaners than I have but have been unable to so far."*

- <u>They're worried</u>: They are as worried about the environment as those women already purchasing a lot of green cleaners. [See Data Deep Dive #17 for more details.]

- <u>They feel their purchases can make a difference</u>: Like so-called *Frequent Greens, Green Aspirants* feel that buying green can help the environment. [See Data Deep Dive #18 for more details.]

- <u>Green cleaners are viewed positively by *Aspirants* on two key product features</u>: Cleaner smell and healthfulness are important to *Green Aspirants* and these women tend to view green cleaners as being better smelling and more healthful than non-green ones. [See Data Deep Dives #19 and #20 for more details.]

So what's stopping *Green Aspirants* from buying more green cleaners?

- <u>Perceived high price of eco-friendly cleaners</u>: *Green Aspirants* most frequently cited price as the barrier preventing them from upping their green cleaner purchases.

- <u>Out of sight, out of mind</u>: *Green Aspirants* in particular often blamed poor green brand awareness and availability on their modest purchasing of green cleaners.

- <u>Perceived inferior effectiveness</u>: A large minority of *Green Aspirants* said that green cleaners' poorer performance vs. that of conventional cleaners prevents them from buying green more. [More about perceived barriers in Data Deep Dive #22]

- <u>Pro-environment attitudes left at the door</u>: *Green Aspirants* often worry about the environment and feel their purchases can make a difference but only about a quarter say they often think about cleaners' environmental impact when buying cleaners. [See Data Deep Dive #20 for more details.]

So how can you convert green attitudes into green purchases?

- Don't price your products out of the reach of *Green Aspirants*.

- Make *Green Aspirants* aware of your brands and make your brands available to them.

- Establish your cleaner's **effectiveness** *bona fides.*

- Show how your products empower *Green Aspirants* to make the environments in their personal lives as well as the one on Planet Earth more healthful, allaying their worries.

  ○ Build a case for the healthfulness of your products **inside** the home.

  ○ Build a case for the healthfulness of your products **outside** the home. An environmental message could resonate with these women if you make your green products part of their consideration set by also addressing *Green Aspirants'* concerns about sustainable brand price, effectiveness, and accessibility.

- Inform these women about your green products through favorable reviews by respected third parties (e.g., *Consumer Reports*, scientists, newspaper/magazine articles) as well as compelling information from you.

Data Deep Dive #21

Green Intention Group Composition - Region

Region	Total Population (n= 628)	Status Quo's (n=332)	Green Aspirants (n=160)	Frequent Greens (n=136)
		A	B	C
West	22.4%	20.7%ₐ	22.5%ₐ	26.4%ₐ
Midwest	21.9%	21.2%ₐ	26.7%ₐ	18.1%ₐ
South	36.9%	40.5%ₐ	30.0%ₐ	36.1%ₐ
Northeast	18.8%	17.6%ₐ	20.8%ₐ	19.4%ₐ
	100.0%	100.0%	100.0%	100.0%

Results are based on two-sided tests with significance level 0.05. For each significant pair, the key of the category with the smaller column proportion appears under the category with the larger column proportion. Tests are adjusted for all pairwise comparisons within a row of each innermost subtable using the Bonferroni correction.

Green Intention Group Composition – Race/Ethnicity

Race/Ethnicity	Total Population (n= 628)	Status Quo's (n=332)	Green Aspirants (n=160)	Frequent Greens (n=136)
		A	B	C
Caucasian	58.8%	61.4%ₐ	55.4%ₐ	56.6%ₐ
Hispanic	15.3%	14.3%ₐ	18.7%ₐ	13.7%ₐ
African/Caribbean-American	16.2%	16.1%ₐ	13.8%ₐ	19.3%ₐ
Asian/Other	9.7%	8.3%ₐ	12.0%ₐ	10.5%ₐ
	100.0%	100.0%	100.0%	100.0%

Results are based on two-sided tests with significance level 0.05. For each significant pair, the key of the category with the smaller column proportion appears under the category with the larger column proportion. Tests are adjusted for all pairwise comparisons within a row of each innermost subtable using the Bonferroni correction.

Green Intention Group Composition – Age

	Total Population (n= 628)	Status Quo's (n=332)	Green Aspirants (n=160)	Frequent Greens (n=136)
Age		A	B	C
22-34	25.0%	25.6%$_a$	26.8%$_a$	21.5%$_a$
35-44	20.7%	21.4%$_a$	19.8%$_a$	19.7%$_a$
45-54	24.2%	20.4%$_a$	31.2%$_b$	25.5%$_{a,b}$
55-79	30.1%	32.6%$_a$	22.1%$_a$	33.3%$_a$
	100.0%	100.0%	100.0%	100.0%

Results are based on two-sided tests with significance level 0.05. For each signifi-cant pair, the key of the category with the smaller column proportion appears under the category with the larger column proportion. Tests are adjusted for all pairwise comparisons within a row of each innermost subtable using the Bonferroni correction

Green Intention Group Composition - Marital Status

	Total Population (n= 628)	Status Quo's (n=332)	Green Aspirants (n=160)	Frequent Greens (n=136)
Marital status		A	B	C
Married	56.2%	56.6%$_a$	60.8%$_a$	50.0%$_a$
Single	21.6%	23.4%$_a$	21.4%$_a$	17.4%$_a$
Divorced	15.5%	13.7%$_a$	15.4%$_a$	19.7%$_a$
Widowed	6.7%	6.2%$_a$	2.4%$_a$	12.9%$_b$
	100.0%	100.0%	100.0%	100.0%

Results are based on two-sided tests with significance level 0.05. For each signifi-cant pair, the key of the category with the smaller column proportion appears under the category with the larger column proportion. Tests are adjusted for all pairwise comparisons within a row of each innermost subtable using the Bonferroni correction

 ## Data Deep Dive #22

Barriers to Green Household Cleaner Purchase among Green Intention Groups

% agreeing with barrier	Barrier Type*	Total Population (n=615)	Status Quo's (n=332)	Green Aspirants (n=160)	Frequent Greens (n=123)
			A	B	C
Green household cleaners are too expensive	P	55.7%	56.4%$_a$	64.0%$_a$	42.9%$_b$
Green household cleaners don't work as well.	Q	34.3%	34.5%$_a$	39.6%$_a$	27.1%$_a$
Green household cleaners are hard to find.	A	31.2%	23.8%$_a$	46.6%$_b$	31.0%$_a$
I like the 'non-green' cleaners I already use.	Q	30.5%	34.7%$_a$	28.2%$_{a,b}$	22.3%$_b$
I'm not aware of many green household cleaners.	A	28.2%	25.2%$_a$	38.4%$_b$	23.2%$_a$
The variety of green household cleaners is poor.	A	24.1%	22.2%$_a$	33.1%$_b$	17.6%$_a$
Not sure green cleaners are better for health.	S	23.6%	23.3%$_a$	27.1%$_a$	20.1%$_a$
Green household cleaners don't smell as good.	Q	18.1%	20.6%$_a$	19.2%$_{a,b}$	10.2%$_b$
I would really have to change my lifestyle.	L	17.5%	15.7%$_a$	19.0%$_a$	20.4%$_a$
Don't trust companies say their cleaners are green.	S	17.2%	14.3%$_a$	20.3%$_a$	21.1%$_a$
I have other things to worry about.	L	16.0%	14.5%$_a$	14.3%$_a$	22.4%$_a$
Buying green cleaners won't make much of a diff.	S	14.4%	13.6%$_a$	16.7%$_a$	13.5%$_a$
Environmental problems aren't as bad as they say.	S	13.1%	12.2%$_a$	15.3%$_a$	13.0%$_a$
My friends & family don't use green cleaners.	L	9.4%	8.5%$_a$	9.0%$_a$	12.2%$_a$
Being green is for hippies.	L	6.2%	5.6%$_a$	8.5%$_a$	4.6%$_a$

Results are based on two-sided tests with significance level 0.05. For each significant pair, the key of the category with the smaller column proportion appears under the category with the larger column proportion. Tests are adjusted for all pairwise comparisons within a row of each innermost subtable using the Bonferroni correction.

*P=Price, Q=Product Quality, A=Access, S=Green Skepticism, L=Lifestyle

CUYAHOGA

Cuyahoga, gone
Let's put our heads together, start a new country up,
Underneath the river bed we burned the river down.
This is where they walked, swam, hunted, danced and sang,
Take a picture here, take a souvenir

-Lyrics from REM's "Cuyahoga"

A news item on my Yahoo homepage today, in homage to Earth Day, reminded me of the days when Cleveland's Cuyahoga River caught fire and Dennis Kucinich was mayor of that city rather than perennial presidential candidate and fodder for late night TV comedians. (Well, he might have been the butt of Johnny Carson's jokes too back in the late '70s.) Oddly enough, those were the good old days for environmentalists when powerful images of filth and neglect galvanized people to demand that the government clean up the environment.

What images do we have now? Melting glaciers and Rocky Mountain lodgepole pines dying from a pine beetle infestation just don't hit most people where they live, like Cleveland or LA. The Yahoo article featured a photo of boat captain that offers cruises down the basically clean Cuyahoga. And Los Angeles residents now contend with peak smog levels that are one-third as high as they were 40 years ago.

And the prodigious snowfalls we northerners have seen in recent seasons don't give us Average Joe's a lot of confidence in the egg-heads who swear that climate change is afoot. "I've got 12 inches of global warming in my driveway for ya', Al Gore!"

Seeing is believing

To mobilize the masses, environmentalists need to present people with lots of compelling images. Art therapist Cathy Malchiodi has said:

> *Sigmund Freud observed that dreams, feelings, and thoughts are experienced predominantly in visual form. Images are part of our earliest experiences, and many of our preverbal thoughts are in images.*

Images are clearly powerful but some images are more powerful than others. I think many people see glaciers and polar bears and think, "yeah, that's a shame but I really have more important things to worry about." Climate change is also starting to affect many people but in a serious, life-altering (even ending) way mainly in other parts of the world. We're now seeing pictures of Kenyan farmers and their children that are suffering from famine because the rainy season hasn't shown up in three years.

Alright, the skeptic says, we've been bombarded by pictures of suffering Africans for years and they may not get the reaction out of people they once did. Well, let's look at the United States then. American gardeners are also experiencing climate change firsthand as the USDA gardening zone maps that spell out what regions are safe for various plants continually change. Massachusetts oranges anyone? And hikers out West have seen their favorite hiking spots laid waste by the aforementioned beetles.

And if you're the indoors type and can't bring your eyes to places where climate change is evident, don't worry, climate change has come to your eyes. Many say that the hellish allergy seasons we've had recently are tied to climate change.

So why isn't all this ocular evidence sinking into our national subconscious more? Are the signs of climate change too subtle? (My red, itchy eyes beg to differ) Or is their link with climate change too subtle? Or is the link not believed by many? Yes, yes, and yes.

Well if visual reminders don't work, perhaps auditory ones will. Michael Stipe, do you have another hooky song about the environment in you?

Paging Jared

Dear Jared:

How have you been doing? Still svelte? It's been awhile since you were a constant presence on our TVs with your tale of how a two Subway subs-a-day diet helped you lose a whopping 245 pounds. The exercise you added to your daily routine didn't hurt either. You were an inspiration to millions of overweight Americans. In fact, Subway says that thousands of people wrote the company to tell of their weight loss, with a total loss of 160,000 pounds. The company's site informs us that this is equal to 10,000 marching band tubas!

Subway made a lot of money from your weight loss. Your work on behalf of the company was a smashing success, and Subway's 2000 sales exceeded those of the previous year by 18 percent. In 2001, they rose another 16% and you became a well-recognized national phenomenon. Subway's since moved on to promoting Five Dollar Footlongs but I hear that you continue speaking on

Subway's behalf. Jared, you're also quite a mensch. Rumor has it that you started the Jared Foundation to combat childhood obesity. Very nice.

A modest proposal

Jared, life's been pretty good to you and you've certainly given back. Also, I know Subway still keeps you busy traveling 200 days a year but if you have some spare time, it would be great if you could help the environment too. I know, asking one man to tackle obesity and our environmental problems is a tall order but you're a natural. I see that you try to eat organic produce when you can. In addition, your employer has a sustainability program called "Eat Fresh. Live Green." So you have at least dipped a toe into the sustainable swimming pool.

"I'm the obesity guy, not the green guy," you might protest. No, Jared you're The Every Guy. I'm sorry but Brad Pitt and Leonardo DiCaprio just don't cut it. We regular guys relate as well to them as we do to the oil-soaked pelicans and dolphins that darken our TV screens [note: blog post was written during the BP oil spill cleanup]. But Jared, *you* we relate to. If you committed to a green lifestyle, think of the possibilities. Maybe we'd get off our fossil fuel-burning butts like when you made us put down our Krispy Kremes and get out of our Barcaloungers a decade ago.

Green Jared imagined

You turn your home green with the help of several sustainable home product manufacturers. From your house's paint to its flooring to the food in your refrigerator, low impact choices will be everywhere. These companies get free advertising and you get some wonderful gifts for your impending nuptials. However, your going green isn't going to be enough by itself to get the rest of us to take the plunge. You have to show us the benefits. When you restricted your diet to Subway subs and lost all that weight, the potential benefit of eating Subway subs was made abundantly clear.

This is definitely going to be a bigger challenge. There will be no irrefutable before-and-after pictures you can produce to show the benefits of going green. How about a before-and-after estimate of your home's carbon footprint then?

However, there might also be health benefits that you can document such as keeping your weight off with all the organic produce you're eating. Also, maybe you and your future wife will have fewer respiratory problems from the lack of paints containing VOCs (volatile organic compounds) and the use of less toxic cleaning products. Keep a journal and see if you notice any other positive health effects of going green.

And let's talk money. Alright, you're getting all these green goodies for free; so rebates and tax breaks may not be in the offing for you. However, you should see your utility bills go down and you may be able to spend less time and money maintaining your home. When you go to resell your home, it should be able to fetch a higher price than a conventional one. And let's not forget those sponsoring companies that might be eager to pay you to work your pr magic for their products.

Besides being healthier and more budget-friendly, a green home may also be more comfortable since heating and cooling will be better distributed throughout the house. And have you seen some of these green buildings? They are pretty easy on the eyes too.

And then there are the intangible benefits to your psyche. Perhaps you'll feel the satisfaction that comes from doing your part to lessen your impact on the environment. And the patriot in you might get a kick from denying revenues to nations that export oil and a hatred of the US.

Will all this lead to a happier, healthier, more fulfilled Jared? Just maybe. After all, you've already seen the benefits of living by the adage "less is more."

All the best,
Jeff Dubin

IV

GIVE HEALTHFULNESS A CHANCE

SHOULD GREEN MARKETERS TAKE A PAGE FROM PHARMA'S PLAYBOOK?

"I have a son who when he was younger had respiratory issues so I would try to keep things as natural as I could for him. I think if you are keeping a clean surface, you are able to do that without all the chemicals."

– 45 year-old woman, Dallas

"I'm sensitive. I get light-headed, feel like I'm suffocating, and I have bad allergies. I will move to other products like Simple Green. It works and smells clean but is not overpowering."

– 59 year-old woman, Philadelphia

These quotes from interviewees in a recent marketing research study conducted by Green Meridian point to something many consumers know. If you or another member of your household has bad allergies or asthma, then conventional cleaning products are a no-no.

In addition, scientific evidence of the harmful nature of toxic cleaners is mounting. A recent article in the *Annals of Allergy, Asthma & Immunology* says house cleaning may make one's asthma worse. Article author Jonathan A. Bernstein, M.D., of the University of Cincinnati's College of Medicine says, "Women with asthma should be routinely interviewed as to whether they clean their home and cautioned about the potential respiratory health effects of these activities."

Children are seen as particularly vulnerable to the chemicals in cleaners. Air pollution testing conducted for the Environmental Working Group (EWG) revealed that cleaning supplies used in 13 key California school districts can cloud classroom air with more than 450 distinct toxic contaminants, including chemical agents linked to asthma and cancer.

Asthma in children has become a particularly worrisome issue as its prevalence has increased dramatically recently, particularly in low income urban areas. According to a recently published study by researchers at George Washington University, in 2008 1 in every 7 children – or 10.2 million – had asthma.

So why aren't green cleaners winning?
There are many reasons why conventional cleaners still have a commanding share of the market:

- The oft-perceived higher price of green brands [See Data Deep Dive #3A for more details]

- Low awareness of many green brands [See Data Deep Dives #4, 6, and 10 for more details]

- Consumer loyalty to tried-and-true cleaning products [See Data Deep Dive #6]

- A belief that green products don't work as well. When it comes to cleaning products, many consumers feel that harsh smells and teary eyes are the price you have to pay to get a germ-free home. In this respect, green cleaners are sometimes seen as having a serious health *liability* since they are unable to disinfect like their more toxic brethren. Especially with the recent H1N1 outbreak, killing germs is seen as Job #1 of cleaning products. [See Data Deep Dive #2 for more details]

- Many people simply don't have chemical sensitivities other than an occasional tearing of the eyes or short-lived choking when they get a strong whiff of a powerful cleaning product

Still, why can't green cleaner marketers be more aggressive in their health claims?

Let's look at some of the factors that may be holding them back.

For starters, makers of green cleaners walk a tightrope. If they are too aggressive in marketing their products' health superiority, conventional cleaner manufacturers can cite green cleaners' lack of disinfecting ability. Recently S.C. Johnson, maker of Fantastik, accused Clorox of being misleading in its claim that its GreenWorks product line works as well as conventional cleaners. The National Advertising Division (NAD) of the Council of Better Business Bureaus agreed with S.C. Johnson and recommended that Clorox discontinue its claims or modify them to state a "more qualified message" because GreenWorks did not perform as well on the "toughest grease" and *did not disinfect like many traditional cleaners.*

And speaking of Clorox, how much hay should the makers of Clorox bleach make about the dangers of traditional cleaning agents? This is yet another tightrope that companies which make both more established conventional cleaners and newer green products must walk.

And what about the "pure green" companies, like the Methods and Seventh Generations, that aren't marketing green products side-by-side with conventional ones? Even they have been cautious in making health claims. Method's *People against Dirty* campaign focuses more on remedying the perceived inability of non-green cleaners to effectively clean than on the health benefits of using Method cleaners. Seventh Generation, however, dove into the healthy home theme in its *Protecting Planet Home* ad campaign but the advertising was spare on specific health benefits.

Why not do something harder hitting? Well, there's the afore-mentioned Achilles heel of not being able to disinfect. Seventh Generation, though, would seem to have that problem licked with its new line of plant-based disinfectants but Method and other cleaners still have that shortcoming. Then there are regulatory constraints on what health benefits can legally be claimed in advertising. And finally the answers to some key strategic marketing questions may militate against more emphasis on their products' health benefits:

- Where does product healthfulness rank among product features in terms of importance to consumers?

- Should our advertising be more positive or negative in tone?

- By trumpeting health benefits too loudly, do I risk niching the product as being only for consumers with respiratory problems?

Sorry, but I can't help but feel that green marketers are leaving something on the table.

Learning from Pfizer

We can debate whether or not green cleaner manufacturers should play up their products' health benefits more with consumers. It's clear that green cleaner manufacturers are at least starting to talk with consumers about the health benefits of their products.

But what about doctors, nurses, pharmacists, chiropractors, and other healthcare providers? Allergies, asthma, and other respiratory problems certainly occupy a significant share of healthcare providers' time and energy. And data – the real peer-reviewed data that professionals respect – is growing that a key trigger of respiratory problems are the chemicals found in many cleaning agents.

How many healthcare professionals are seeing the data?

In launching its line of plant-based disinfectants, Seventh Generation noted the laudatory words of Stanford pediatrician Dr. Alan Greene, "It is increasingly important to protect our health and that of our children by implementing good hygiene practices and using disinfectants around the home that are effective without the use of harsh chemicals. Seventh Generation's disinfectants are a historic product introduction for consumers and the industry."

Yet Dr. Greene was talking primarily to consumers. Is Seventh Generation also sponsoring Dr. Greene talks at the annual meetings of the American Academy of Allergy, Asthma & Immunology or the American Academy of Pediatrics?

The green marketer may retort, "Yeah, but we're a consumer products company not a drug company. We don't have Merck's money or expertise in sponsoring medical education and in the big picture, doctors play a relatively small role in the purchase of our products."

With as many as 45 million Americans suffering from chemical sensitivity and 34 million suffering from asthma, shouldn't doctors play a larger role? And jaded doctors who have been heavily marketed to by drug companies for years might welcome fresh new information they haven't seen before.

Rx FOR THE BETROTHED (WALMART & SEVENTH GENERATION)

A n unusual pairing, although not quite as strange as that of Julia Roberts and Lyle Lovett in the 90s, was announced on Monday (7/26/10). Walmart has decided to carry Seventh Generation products. For a company with $150 million in 2009 sales, this decision can potentially multiply Seventh Generation's revenues.

To make the marriage work, Seventh Generation and Walmart need to overcome two challenges:

1. **Walmart customers need to become aware of Seventh Generation products**. When I showed mainstream women Seventh Generation product samples in a marketing research study Green Meridian did, many responded as if

they were looking at moon rocks. Seventh Generation and Walmart will have to aggressively work to raise women's awareness of the products, despite SG's imminent presence on the shelves of thousands of Walmart's.

2. **Seventh Generation has to give mainstream women compelling reasons to switch from their current cleaning products.** This is going to involve education. Lowering prices to at or near parity with leading brands, as Seventh Generation has done, gets a green brand only so far. Seventh Generation will have to convince women that its products work at least as well as the cleaning products they currently use and that using SG offers significant health advantages.

Jeffrey Hollender, Seventh Generation's founder and former Chief Inspired Protagonist, acknowledged that making it onto Walmart's shelves is only the first step:

> *New access to our products will do some of this work, but not all of it. We're also partnering with Walmart to advance our shared sustainability goals in part through participation in a Walmart working group focused on improving the safety of chemical-intensive products, and we'll be helping Walmart educate shoppers about why the product choices they make matter so very much.*

Before I go further, let me state that the stereotype of Walmart's shoppers as being working class people with less education is a bit outdated as the recession has forced many more well off, better educated people to venture into Walmart for the first time. However, it is probably not a stretch to say that Walmart's customers overall are less educated, less eco-oriented, and less wealthy than the customers of Seventh Generation's traditional haunts, upmarket sophisticated stores such as Whole Foods. Although Seventh Generation's experience selling products to Target and traditional supermarket customers should be good preparation,

Seventh Generation faces a large challenge in succeeding at the level Walmart will demand.

Try it, your body will like it

So how does the pride of Burlington succeed in Middle America? I asked Chicago-based shopper marketing expert Nancy Alexandroff what she would advise Seventh Generation. Here's what she said:

> *I think there are two key success factors for Seventh Generation: Generate awareness followed by lowering the perceived risk. Awareness can be generated using targeted in-store media. Usually awareness is best created by mass media but do they have the money for extensive TV? I'm not sure. Radio's an option – drive time or a.m. in high CDI (category development index) markets. Radio can be affordable and a good way to reach mainstream green moms who are driving the kids around town.*
>
> *Then, lowering the perceived risk of purchasing is best done by putting the product either on deal or offering a coupon, or both. The coupon has to be a cents off coupon, and the purchase requirement has to be easily met (one bottle). No "buy one, get one" deals. Who wants to take the chance of getting stuck with TWO bottles of something that you end up not liking?*

A coupon or discount may lower the barrier to trial but Seventh Generation also needs to give consumers a reason to try their products in the first place. How does Seventh Generation succeed in its proclaimed goal of "helping Walmart educate shoppers about why the product choices they make matter so very much" and convincing shoppers that their products are better choices?

Convincing consumers Seventh Generation products work can result from successful product trial but convincing them that

Seventh Generation products are meaningfully healthier is a more complex sell. The company fortunately has experience in this area and already has a tool to help consumers make sense of confusing product labels. Their Label Reading Guide explains why some of those hard to pronounce ingredients may be hurting them, their families, and the environment.

In addition, Seventh Generation's *7Gen Blog* provides a platform to both educate and interact with customers. Some interested Walmart shoppers might find their way to the *7Gen Blog*. Finally, Walmart will likely provide opportunities for Seventh Generation to educate consumers in the store.

A boost for green from the people in white

While a formidable consumer education campaign can be crafted out of a combination of social, mass, and in-store media, still I feel that such an educational effort will be lost on a lot of shoppers. In-store education is challenging with all the distractions of a busy retail environment. And once the shopper leaves the store, you've got the motivation barrier. How many shoppers will take the time to peruse the informative online materials provided by Seventh Generation and others?

That's where doctors come in. Huh? Yes doctors, namely pediatricians, gynecologists, family practice doctors, internists, and allergists. And the nurse practitioners, physician assistants, and RNs that work with them. Although the eco-friendliness of Seventh's Generation's products is a nice bonus, Green Meridian's research shows that it is rarely a significant factor in mainstream women's household cleaner selection process. There is a group of mainstream women that want to green up though and many of these women *do consider* cleaner <u>healthfulness</u> when shopping.

Teaching green to healthcare providers

Asking a healthcare provider which products are safe to use is often preferred by many women to parsing large amounts of fairly technical information on one's own on the Internet. Even if a woman is motivated enough to do the research, it's not easy for a layperson to separate what's meaningful from what's not for a specific household situation. But forget about *meaningful*. Laypeople have trouble just figuring out what's *credible*.

Make no mistake. Conversations between patients (or their parents) and doctors about the toxicity of products brought into the home are already happening. But how well equipped are doctors to have these conversations? The science is evolving and the wide scope of many medical professionals' practices, particularly primary care ones, requires practitioners to stay current on a vast array of conditions. They only have so much bandwidth available to understanding the threats posed by household products. Doctors, nurse practitioners, physician assistants, and RNs need some help.

I must have missed this class in med school

Before Seventh Generation and others can educate healthcare providers about the health implications of ingredients in household cleaners, they first need to *understand* how much doctors currently know about cleaner ingredients. To what extent do doctors and others know about the ties between various cleaner ingredients and health risks? What types of healthcare providers know more? What types know less? Do they even *believe* cleaner ingredients pose a significant health risk? Once companies have this baseline understanding of providers' knowledge and perceptions, they can then set education goals.

What do you think? Should makers of green household products spend valuable promotional resources on educating doctors and nurses?

REIGNITING THE PASSION

I n this year of fiery political passions, the word "revolt" is in the air. However, I think *Ad Age* inhaled an extra whiff of the zeitgeist and incorrectly applied the term to consumers supposedly cooling in their ardor for green products. *"Has Green Stopped Giving? Seeds of Consumer Revolt Sprouting against Some Environmentally Friendly Product Lines"* trumpeted the headline of a recent *Ad Age* article. A couple paragraphs into the article, the author quotes Timothy Kenyon, director of GfK Roper's Green Gauge study who more judiciously described the current situation as "green fatigue."

Yes, some green product lines, such as Clorox' Green Works and SC Johnson's Nature's Source have faced setbacks. And yes, Frito-Lay has had to rejigger the compostable SunChips bag that loudly announced its presence every time you handled it. But green products have had some victories too lately. What about Seventh Generation products getting access to the shelves of 1,500 Walmart stores? And the article mentions "Method's sales hike so far this year after a tough 2009." Revolt? No. Fatigue? Maybe.

Fatigue doesn't quite nail it for me though. It implies that there are people who were once excited by green that are now onto something else. I think you can say that about journalists and pundits who helped fan the flames of green hype but not consumers. The Ad Age article talks about the "Gartner hype curve," with the green market moving from the "'peak of inflated expectations" to the "trough of disillusionment" but I think that applies more to bloggers (guilty as charged) than to American shoppers.

So why is fatigue an incorrect term to use with consumers? Because the vast majority of consumers didn't have "green fever" to begin with. They had nothing against green products per se, but green just wasn't on their radar. And if green products weren't on consumers' radar in 2009, after many more months of an anemic economy, they're certainly not on most consumers' radar now. Green marketers picked the lower hanging fruit (i.e., easy to acquire consumers) but the higher fruit may be, if not out of reach, then in need of a tall, sturdy ladder and advanced picking techniques to get.

So what should we call the current green marketing situation *the green slackening?* Or *the green reality check?*

Green Marketing 3.0 for green's blues

Green marketing maven Jacquie Ottman has blogged that "Over time, mainstream companies entering the [green] market espoused what I call the 'planets, babies and daisies' approach (despite doing otherwise on established brands) mostly likely believing such imagery represented a price of entry into a market they didn't understand and were not quite comfortable playing in." Let's call the "planets, babies, and daisies" approach **Green Marketing 1.0**.

So, what's **Green Marketing 2.0**? Jacquie again provides a good definition: "Now such brands as Green Works or Tide Coldwater are realizing that the name of the game is doing what they do naturally—leading with messages of primary benefits, while bringing in environmental messages as secondary." By primary benefits, Jacquie means the main product features people consider when buying a product. With detergents, it's going to be cleaning ability and price. So an environmental message can be seen as a tie-breaker for many mainstream consumers. And for other mainstream consumers, products' relative greenness is a total non-factor in their purchase decisions for a wide variety of reasons including a perception that buying green has no relevance to their lives.

Must a product's environmental friendliness forever be relegated to the role of tie-breaker at best in mainstream consumers' minds? Maybe not. I say let's revisit Jacquie's "planets, babies, and daisies" but don't throw the baby out with the planets and daisies. To really succeed on a wide scale in America, green products either need to establish their superiority on conventional, non-green product features such as effectiveness or price (very tough) or make green more relevant to people's everyday lives (tough but not impossible). If green marketers can build the case for how their products are healthier, **then the greenness of a product becomes a primary benefit rather than a secondary one** and the higher hanging fruit now becomes more attainable. That's **Green Marketing 3.0.**

Green Marketing 2.0 has helped green products find new audiences by creating green products that work and are affordable but we may be starting to see the limits of this approach, at least in the current environment. To ascend to the next level where green really tips in its appeal to the mass market will require Green Marketing 3.0, where buying green is tied to the health of *both* humans and polar bears.

V

ABOUT THE
SUSTAINABILITY IN THE
MAINSTREAM STUDY

METHODOLOGY

Markets Studied

- Personal care products: Soaps, deodorants, perfumes, shampoos, conditioners, hair styling products, toothpaste and other oral care products, makeup, lipstick

- Household cleaners: Bathroom cleaners, kitchen cleaners, furniture polish and dusting products, floor cleaners and waxes, laundry detergents

Quantitative Survey

- 30-minute online survey was fielded with 628 women during September 2009.

- Survey explored current and future green purchasing behavior, drivers of and barriers to green purchasing, underlying attitudes, and preferred ways to obtain information on green products.

In-Person Depth Interviews

- Twenty-five in-person 45-minute interviews were conducted with women in September 2009.

- Respondents varied on demographics and green purchasing levels

- Women interviewed in Bala Cynwyd, PA (suburban Philadelphia) and Dallas, TX.

Telephone Depth Interviews

- Ten 30-minute telephone interviews were conducted with women in December 2009.

- Respondents currently buy low to moderate quantities of green products but would like to buy more.

- Main objective was to further delve into green product perceptions of this group.

APPENDIX

GREEN PURCHASING VS. GREEN INTENTION GROUPS

Rules for Assigning Women to *Green Purchasing Groups*

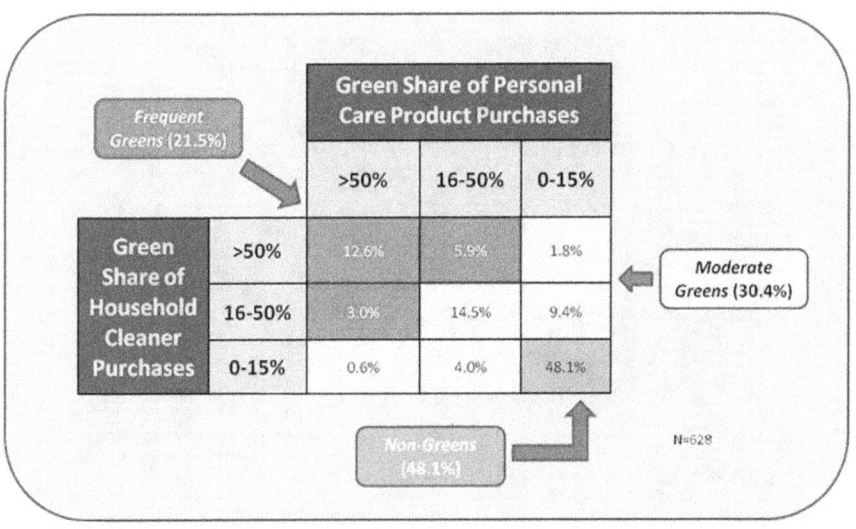

Rules for Assigning Women to *Green Intention Groups*

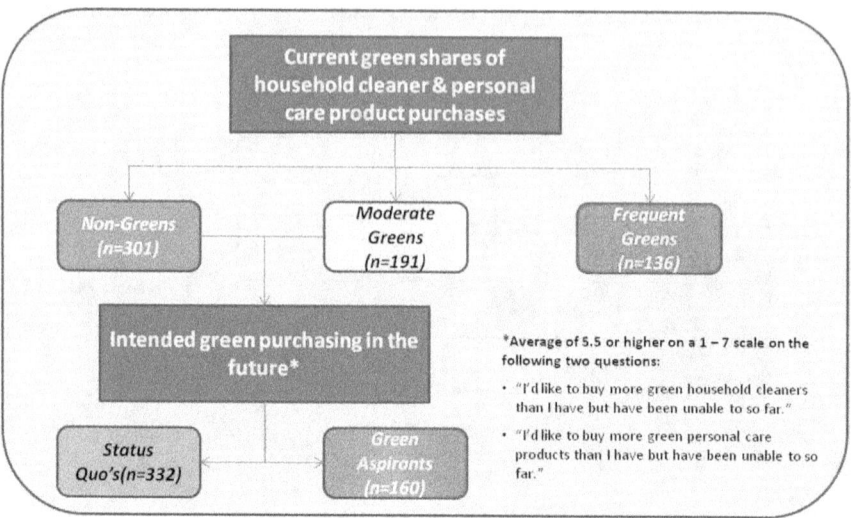

www.ingramcontent.com/pod-product-compliance
Lightning Source LLC
Chambersburg PA
CBHW071224170526
45165CB00003B/977